The Great Big
COOKIE BOOK

The Great Big
COOKIE BOOK

Over 200 recipes for cookies, brownies, scones, bars and biscuits

Hilaire Walden

LORENZ BOOKS

This edition published in 1998 by Lorenz Books
27 West 20th Street, New York, NY 10011

LORENZ BOOKS are available for bulk purchase for sales promotion
and for premium use. For details, write or call the sales director,
Lorenz Books, 27 West 20th Street, New York, NY 10011; (800) 354-9657

© Anness Publishing Limited 1998

Lorenz Books is an imprint of
Anness Publishing Limited

ISBN 1 85967 738 x

Publisher: Joanna Lorenz
Project Editor: Joanne Rippin
Designer: Siân Keogh, Axis Design
Illustrator: Christos Chrysanthou, Axis Design

Printed and bound in Italy

3 5 7 9 10 8 6 4 2

Contents

Introduction

The word cookie has become quite common throughout the world; here we present cookies in their many guises.

The word "cookie" is of Dutch origin, from the word *koekje* meaning little cake. The origins of the British term for cookie, biscuit, are to be found in the word itself: it comes from the French *bis cuit,* meaning twice cooked, and goes back to the days when bakers put slices of newly baked bread back into the oven, so that they dried out completely, becoming something like a rusk. This was really a method of preservation, for it enabled the cookies to be kept for a long time; so long, in fact, that they could be taken as a basic food item, known as "ships biscuits," on long sea voyages.

For many years cooks and housewives continued the practice of drying their biscuits a second time, and it was not until the beginning of the last century that the habit died out. Then both the quality and variety of biscuits that could be made improved dramatically.

Now there are many names and forms for cookies, but usually they are individual, small, crisp baked cakes. We call them cookies when they are sweet, crackers when savory, while in Britain both cookies and crackers are called biscuits. To add to the confusion, we call biscuits what the British generally call scones, while we usually agree on what we call muffins. Happily, the distinctions are blurring, and in this *Great Big Cookie Book* you will find the truth in the baking and tasting of the many cookies, biscuits, crackers, muffins and scones described here.

We have collected cookies from all over the world, family favorites for generations, classic recipes for holidays and celebrations, and national specialties that have crossed many borders, such as Amaretti from Italy, Basbousa from the Middle East and Oatcakes from Scotland. Here you will find a homemade cookie for every occasion. And homemade cookies put the store-bought to shame; a batch of cookies ready to come out of the oven will fill your kitchen with a wonderful aroma, followed by the unbeatable taste of your own fresh-baked creation.

Finally, cookies are easy and fun to make. You can make them alone to cheer up a rainy day, or share the enjoyment with your family and friends, especially fun at holiday times. So, turn the pages of this book with anticipation of the many treats to come.

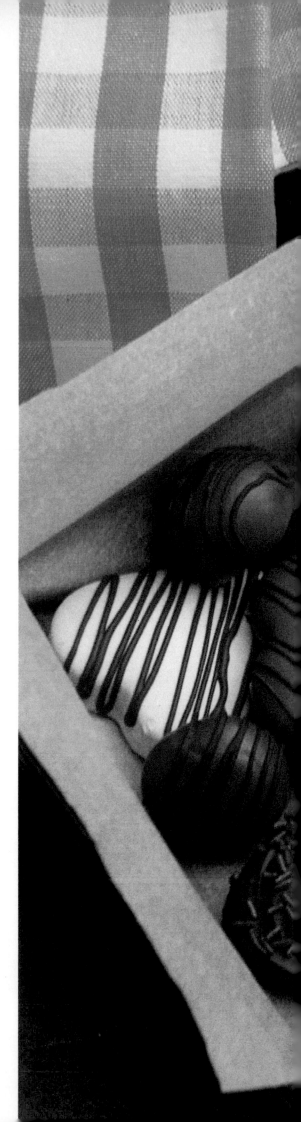

▶ *Cookies are not only ideal for everyday eating or special treats at home; they can also be gift wrapped and given away as a special gift.*

Cookie Tips
& Techniques

Cookies can be made using a wide variety of methods to suit all ranges of ability and to match the time and ingredients available. Most cookies are easy to make and special skills are rarely required. But, as with most things, once you know exactly the right way to do something, it becomes that much quicker, easier and enjoyable, and the results are far more likely to be successful. The following pages in the Cookie Tips & Techniques section provide all the information you will need to make successful cookies every time, with the minimum amount of effort.

You will find advice on choosing the most appropriate ingredients for the particular cookie you are making, and handy tips on how to carry out simple but vital tasks like measuring accurately. There are detailed instructions for all the methods used for making and shaping cookies, including piping the raw mixture, as well as the various methods of melting chocolate. Ideas for making cookies look really attractive are also included, and the way to make piping bags from greaseproof paper is described.

There are also recommendations on storing the cookies so they will remain fresh for as long as possible, plus ideas on how to wrap and present your cookies so they become special gifts with a strong personal feel.

The Pantry

The ingredients for cookie making can be found in most people's pantries and refrigerators.

Chocolate Buy good quality chocolate with at least 50% cocoa solids for baking. Semisweet chocolate gives a distinctive strong, rich flavor while milk chocolate has a sweeter taste. White chocolate often does not contain any cocoa solids and lacks the flavor of true chocolate. It is the most difficult chocolate to melt and has poor setting qualities.

Eggs Eggs should be at room temperature so, if you keep them in the refrigerator, remove the number you want at least 30 minutes before making a recipe.

Flours Flour provides the structure that makes the cookies. Always sift flour. Not only will this remove any lumps, which are rare nowadays, but it lightens the flour by incorporating air and makes it easier to mix in.

Self-rising flour has rising agents added and is the type of flour most usually used in straightforward cookies that need to rise.

All-purpose flour is used when rising is considered a fault, as when making shortbread. Rich or heavy mixtures that should be raised also often call for all-purpose flour plus additional rising agents in the specific proportions required for the particular recipe.

Wholewheat flour adds more flavor than white flour and is the healthier option but does produce denser cookies. When lightness is important extra rising agents should be added. Some recipes work well with a mixture of white and whole wheat flour.

Dried fruits Today, most dried fruits are dried by artificial heat rather than by the sun, and are treated with sulphur dioxide to help their preservation. Oils are sometimes sprayed onto the fruit to give it a shiny appearance and to prevent it from sticking. Try to buy fruit that has been coated with vegetable oils, not mineral oils.

Butter and margarine Butter gives the best flavor to cookies and should be used whenever possible, especially when there is a high fat content, as in shortbread. However, it can be used interchangeably with hard margarine. Butter or margarine to be used for creaming with sugar needs to be at room temperature and softened. For rubbing in, it should be at a cool room temperature, not refrigerator hard, and chopped quite finely.

Soft margarine is really only suitable for making cookies by the all-in-one method and when the fat has to be melted.

Candied fruits Wash candied fruits before using them to remove the syrupy coating, then dry thoroughly.

Spices Ground cinnamon, ginger, apple pie or pumpkin pie spice, nutmeg and cloves may be used in cookies. All spices should be as fresh as possible. Buy in small quantities, and keep in a cool, dark, dry place.

Honey Honey adds its own distinctive flavor to cookies. It contains 17% water so you will need to use slightly more honey than sugar, and reduce the amounts of the other liquids used. Use honey within a few months of opening, and keep in a cool, dark, dry place.

Sugars Granulated sugar is the best sweetener to use for the creaming method because the crystals dissolve easily and quickly when creamed with the fat. Granulated sugar can also be used for rubbed-in mixtures and when the sugar is heated with the fat or liquid until it dissolves. Confectioners' sugar appears in the ingredients for some cookie recipes where it is important that the sugar dissolves very readily. Demerara sugar can be used when the sugar is dissolved over heat before being added to the dry ingredients. Soft light and dark brown sugars are used when a richer flavor and color are called for. Raw sugar is unrefined sugar which is uncolored and pure.

Nuts Nuts become rancid if stored for too long, in the light or at too high a temperature, so only buy in amounts that you will use within 1-2 months and keep them in an airtight container in a cool, dark cupboard. Alternatively, freeze them for up to 1 year.

Equipment

A delightful aspect of cookie making is that it requires a minimum of special equipment.

You can make a wide range of cookies with just a mixing bowl, measures or weights, a wooden spoon, a baking sheet and a wire rack. Only a few items are needed to extend the range much further. Many supermarkets now sell all you will need for cookie making.

Baking sheets Use good-quality sturdy sheets; thin, cheap sheets will buckle with time. Cheap sheets also heat more quickly so cookies are liable to cook quickly, brown and stick to them more readily. Nonstick sheets, of course, save greasing and lining when called for, greatly reduce sticking and cut down on washing up.

Cannelle knife This tool is great for carving stripes in the skin of citrus fruit. Pare off thin strips before slicing the fruit to make an attractive edge.

Cutters Cutters are available in many different shapes and sizes, ranging from simple plain cookie circles to small cutters for *petits fours* and savory cocktail nibbles, to animal shapes, hearts and flowers. For best results, the important criterion that applies to all cutters is that they should be sharp to give a good, clear, outline. This really means that they should be made from metal; plastic cutters tend to compress the cut edges.

To use a cutter, press down firmly on the cutter so that it cuts straight down right through the dough. Then lift up the cutter, without twisting it.

If you want to cut out a shape for which you do not have a cutter, the thing to do is to make a template, or pattern. This is very easy.

Trace or draw the design onto waxed paper or cardboard and cut it out using scissors. Lay the template on the rolled-out cookie dough. Use the point of a large, sharp knife to carefully cut around the template, taking care not to drag it. With a thin metal spatula, transfer the shape to the prepared baking sheet, without distorting the shape.

Food processor Although food processors save time, their drawback is their very speed; they work so fast that you must be careful not to overmix a mixture. Food processors combine rather than beat ingredients together, so they are not so useful for recipes where lightness is important. Also, many models cannot beat egg whites, and even in those designed for beating, the whites will not become really stiff.

Knives A table knife can be used for the initial stages of cutting in the fat before it is rubbed in. Large, sharp knives are needed for cutting cleanly and efficiently through rolled-out dough or refrigerated dough. Metal spatulas are invaluable for spreading

and smoothing mixtures in cake pans, transferring cut-out cookies to baking sheets before baking and then transferring the baked cookies to a wire rack to cool. They can also be used for spreading icing on cookies.

Measures A set of accurate measuring spoons is vital for measuring 1 tablespoon, 1 teaspoon and fractions of teaspoons. All the amounts given in recipes are for level spoonfuls unless otherwise stated. For liquids, use a heatproof measuring cup, preferably see-through in 1-cup, 2-cup and 4-cup sizes.

Pastry brushes A large pastry brush is very useful for brushing surplus flour from work surfaces and cookie doughs that are being rolled out, and for greasing cake pans. A pastry brush is also needed for brushing on glazes. Buy good-quality brushes with firmly fixed bristles.

Piping bags and nozzles A medium icing bag with a selection of nozzles is very useful to have for piping uncooked cookie dough and for decorating cookies after baking. Use small disposable icing bags for chocolate or icing, where a fine line is required.

Rolling pin Rolling pins made of wood are the most common, but you can now buy marble or even plastic ones which are considered to be more hygienic.

Scales A good set of scales is essential for successful cookie making. Whether you use spring balance, modern electronic or old-fashioned balanced scales with a set of weights, test them frequently for accuracy by putting something on them which has the weight printed on it.

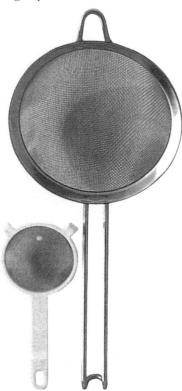

Sieves If possible have a set of strong sieves in 2 or 3 different sizes.

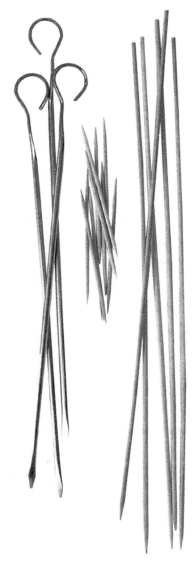

Skewers and toothpicks Either of these can be used for testing whether cookie mixtures are cooked.

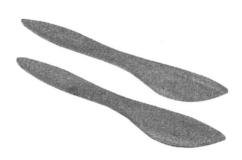

Spatulas A flexible rubber spatula is indispensable for scraping every last morsel from the mixing bowl onto the baking sheet.

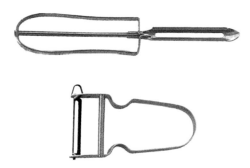

Swivel-blade peelers Both long-handled and broad-handled peelers are the best tools for peeling fruit.

Tea strainer A tea strainer will come in handy for sifting icing sugar over cookies as a last-minute decoration.

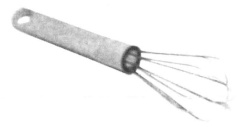

Whisk Use either a wire balloon whisk or a rotary whisk for beating eggs together. It is a good idea to have two sizes of balloon whisks, to suit the amount of mixture.

Zester Ideal for citrus fruit, a zester has the same function as a cannelle knife but produces a row of thin stripes.

Cookie Tips & Techniques

Measuring ingredients

Cooks with years of experience may not need to measure ingredients, but if you are a beginner or are trying a new recipe for the first time, it is best to follow instructions carefully. Also, measuring ingredients precisely will ensure consistent results.

1 For liquids measured in cups or pints: use a glass or clear plastic measuring cup. Put it on a flat surface and pour in the liquid. Bend down and check that the liquid is level with the marking on the cup, as specified in the recipe.

2 For liquids measured in spoons: pour the liquid into the measuring spoon, to the brim, and then pour it into the mixing bowl. Do not hold the spoon over the bowl when measuring because some liquid may overflow.

3 For measuring dry ingredients in a spoon: fill the spoon, scooping up the ingredient. Level the surface to the rim of the spoon, using the straight edge of a knife.

4 For measuring dry ingredients by weight: scoop or pour onto the scales, watching the dial or reading carefully. Balance scales give more accurate readings than spring scales.

5 For measuring syrups: grease the inside of a measuring cup before pouring in the required weight of syrup.

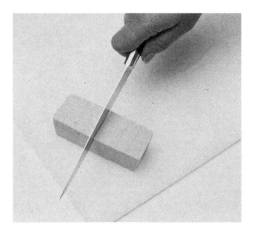

6 For measuring butter: cut with a sharp knife and weigh, or cut off the specified amount following the markings on the wrapping paper.

Making cookies by the rubbing in method

Plain cookies are usually made by rubbing the fat into the flour. For this, the fat, whether butter, margarine or lard, should be neither rock hard from the refrigerator, nor too warm. It is first chopped into small pieces, then added to the dry ingredients in a bowl. The mixture is lifted high and the lumps of fat rubbed between the fingertips as the mixture is allowed to fall back into the bowl.

1 Sift the flour into a bowl, adding the raising agents, salt and any sugar or spices and mix them evenly.

2 Stir in any other dry ingredients; combine the oats or other cereal, or coconut. Add the butter or margarine, cut into pieces.

3 Sprinkle the liquid ingredients (water, cream, milk, buttermilk or beaten egg) over the mixture.

4 Stir with a fork until the dry ingredients are thoroughly moistened and will come together in a ball of fairly soft dough in the center of the bowl.

5 Press the dough into a ball. If it is too dry to form a dough, add some extra water.

6 Turn the dough onto a lightly floured surface. Knead very lightly, folding and pressing, to mix evenly – about 30 seconds. Wrap the ball of dough in plastic wrap or waxed paper and chill it for at least 30 minutes.

Making cookies by the creaming method

To make cookies by the creaming method, the fat and sugar are "creamed" – or beaten – together before the eggs and dry ingredients are added. The fat (usually butter or margarine) should be soft enough to be beaten so, if necessary, remove it from the refrigerator and leave for at least 30 minutes. For best results, the eggs should be at room temperature.

1 Sift the flour with the salt, raising agent(s) and any other dry ingredients, such as spices or cocoa powder, into a bowl. Set aside.

2 Put the fat in a large, deep bowl and beat with an electric mixer at medium speed, or a wooden spoon, until the texture is soft and pliable.

3 Add the sugar to the creamed fat gradually. With the mixer at medium-high speed, or using the wooden spoon, beat it into the fat until the mixture is pale and very fluffy. The sugar should be completely incorporated.

5 Add the dry ingredients to the mixture. Beat at low speed just until smoothly combined, or fold in with a large metal spoon.

6 If the recipe calls for any liquid, add it in small portions alternately with portions of the dry ingredients.

7 If the recipe specifies, beat egg whites separately until frothy, add sugar and continue whisking until stiff peaks form. Fold into the mixture.

Making cookies by the all-in-one method

Some cookies are made by an easy all-in-one method where all the ingredients are combined in a bowl and beaten thoroughly. The mixture can also be made in a food processor, but take care not to over-process. A refinement on the all-in-one method is to separate the eggs and make the mixture with the yolks. The whites are whisked separately and then folded in. Soft margarine has to be used.

4 Add the eggs or egg yolks, one at a time, beating well after each addition. Scrape the bowl often so all the ingredients are evenly combined. If the mixture curdles, add 1 tbsp of the measured flour.

1 Sift the flour and any other dry ingredients such as salt, raising agents and spices, into a bowl.

2 Add the liquid ingredients, such as eggs, melted or soft fat, milk or fruit juices, and beat until smooth, with an electric mixer for speed. Pour into the prepared pans and bake as specified in the recipe.

8 Pour the mixture into a prepared cake pan and bake as specified.

Rolling and cutting cookies

A cookie dough that is to be rolled and cut must have the right consistency; if it is too dry it will crumble, crack and be difficult to roll neatly, whereas if it is too wet it will stick when rolled out and will spread during baking.

1 After mixing, knead the cookie dough lightly so it holds together, then wrap it in plastic wrap or waxed paper and chill it for at least 1 hour. To speed the chilling, put the dough in the freezer for 30 minutes. Tap over the dough with a rolling pin to flatten it, then gently roll out the dough with short, light strokes in one direction to the required thickness.

2 Doughs that are stiff enough to roll may be cut with a knife into squares, rectangles, triangles or fingers, or they can be stamped into rounds or fancy shapes using cutters. To prevent sticking, sprinkle the work surface generously with flour or sugar, according to the recipe, before rolling out the dough, and use a floured or sugared rolling pin.

3 Position the floured cutter near the outside edge of the dough and cut out the shape. Continue cutting out shapes, each time placing the cutter close to the cut-out holes, to minimize trimmings. Carefully transfer to the prepared baking sheet. Glaze with beaten egg and sprinkle with nuts, seeds or cheese, if used.

Shaping drop cookies

1 Drop cookies are made from a number of different mixtures, but they invite the use of coarse-textured oats, nuts and dried fruits that cannot be piped through a nozzle. Drop cookies are easy to shape; spoonfuls of mixture are simply dropped onto the prepared baking sheet.

2 Leave plenty of space between the cookies because they spread during cooking. If a mixture is stiff it will have to be spread with the back of a teaspoon or fork, but this is not usually necessary. Drop teaspoons of the mixture onto the prepared baking sheet, spacing them well apart.

Shaping tuiles & cigarettes

Delicate drop cookies, such as Tuiles d'amandes and Brandy Snaps, can be a challenge to the cook. The mixture is particularly thin and a tablespoon or less of flour or liquid can make the difference between success and failure.

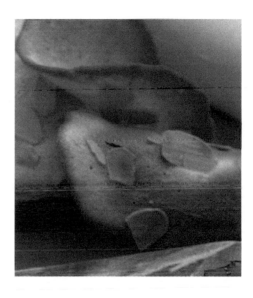

1 Roll spoonfuls of the dough into balls and place 1–2 inches apart on the prepared baking sheets.

2 Bake until golden brown, 8–10 minutes. With a metal spatula transfer to a rolling pin to shape, then leave to cool.

Molding cookies

Doughs that are too rich to roll out can be shaped by hand. Some recipes call for moistening your hands with water before handling the dough, others recommend lightly flouring your hands, or using cocoa powder or sugar.

1 Take walnut-size pieces of dough and roll into smooth balls between the palms of your hands. Set them spaced well apart on the prepared baking sheet.

2 Flatten the balls with the back of the tines of a wetted fork to give a lined effect. Alternatively, the base of a greased glass dipped in superfine or confectioners' sugar can be used.

Making refrigerator cookies

These are so called because the dough must be thoroughly chilled before it can be cut into slices for baking, and also because the dough can be conveniently kept in the refrigerator for up to a week before it is baked. The dough can also be frozen and used straight from the freezer, using a good sharp knife.

Refrigerator cookies are simple to make because the chilled logs are firm and easy to slice. They are also time-saving because you can make the roll ahead and slice off just as many cookies as you need at any time. Use a thin, sharp knife and wet the knife occasionally to help to give a smooth, clean cut.

The thickness of the slices determines the character of baked cookies: very thin slices will bake into thin, crisp cookies; thick slices result in thicker, more chewy cookies. Place 1 inch apart on the baking sheets, which are usually ungreased.

1 Beat together the butter and sugar until light and fluffy. Add the flour in three batches, folding in well between each addition. Add any other ingredients and stir in gently.

2 Divide the dough in half and shape each half into a log about 2 inches in diameter. Wrap in waxed paper and chill overnight. Preheat the oven to 375°F. Lightly grease two baking sheets.

3 Cut the dough logs across into slices about $1/8$ inch thick. Place on the prepared baking sheets. Bake for about 10 minutes, until just golden around the edges. Transfer to a wire rack to cool.

Piping cookies

The mixture for piped cookies needs to be soft enough to pipe, but it should not be too loose or it will spread and lose its shape during baking. You will need a piping bag of an appropriate size and a large nozzle, either plain or star-shaped, depending on the effect you want to produce (obviously, a star nozzle will give a more decorative appearance). Drop the piping nozzle into the piping bag and twist, tucking the bag into the nozzle. This will prevent any filling from leaking out at the bottom.

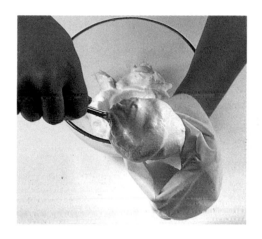

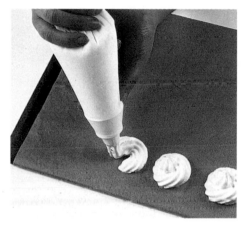

1 Fold the top of the bag over your hand to form a collar, or stand the bag in a tall glass. Add the mixture, scraping the spoon or spatula against your hand or the side of the glass. When the bag is one-half to two-thirds full, twist the top until there is no air left.

2 Hold the twisted end of the bag firmly in one hand. Use the other hand to lightly guide the nozzle. Exert a very firm, steady pressure and start to pipe. The trick is to keep the pressure steady until the design is finished. A sudden squeeze will produce a large blob rather than an even flow.

3 As soon as the shape is complete, stop applying pressure, push down slightly and quickly lift up the nozzle.

4 The bag is kept upright for piping swirls, stars or rosettes, but to make straight lines it is held at an angle.

Making a waxed paper icing bag

Waxed paper icing bags are particularly good for piping small quantities

of icing or when two or more colors of icing are being used at once.

They are also easy to use for any type of icing. The bag can be used without

a piping nozzle for making simple, plain lines, or it can be fitted with any size of nozzle.

It is a good idea to make several of these bags at a time.

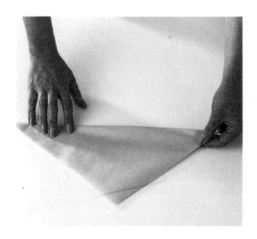

1 Cut a piece of good quality waxed paper to a 10-inch square. Fold in half to form a triangle.

2 Fold the short side of the triangle over to the right-angled corner to form a cone.

3 Holding the cone together with one hand, wrap the long point of the triangle around the paper cone.

Tip To use the bag for piping, do not overfill it; instead, open it carefully and refill it when necessary, taking care not to split it or let it unfold. The filled bag can be kept in a plastic bag for a few hours.

4 Tuck the point of paper inside the cone to secure it. For extra security, clear tape can be used to hold the paper together. Add the icing, then cut a small, straight piece off the end of the bag.

5 For using with a nozzle, cut off the pointed end of the bag and position the nozzle so that it fits snugly into the point before adding the icing.

Cookie Tips & Techniques

Decorating cookies with icing

It is very easy to turn plain cookies into special-looking treats, whether for a children's birthday party or to give as a present to an adult. All that is needed is some icing – you don't even have to do any piping. However, it is a very simple matter to add a little piped icing. There's no need to be adept at icing – the surfaces you will be covering are small so it won't matter if the lines are squiggly.

A very easy way to decorate the tops of cookies is to spread the icing over the top, using a palette knife.

Another very straightforward way to ice the tops of cookies is to just dip them in the icing.

Icing glaze This is like glacé icing but is thinned with egg white so that it sets, making a thin, tangy cookie glaze.

1 tbsp lightly beaten egg white
1 tbsp lemon juice
¼–1 cup confectioners' sugar
Mix the egg white and lemon juice in a bowl. Beat in the confectioners' sugar gradually, until the mixture is smooth with the consistency of thin cream. The icing should coat the back of a spoon.

Stenciling

A simple yet effective way to decorate cookies is to pipe lines of a contrasting color backwards and forwards across the top of the baked cookies. With just a few simple, short lines you can add the finishing touches to some spectacular cookies.

A portion of the raw cookie mixture can be colored then piped over the shaped, but still unbaked cookies, so the design is baked in the cookies.

Stenciling is a fun way to liven up cookies. There are no hard and fast rules – experiment with different templates. Cut a small design or initial out of card and place it over a cookie. Dust the cookie with confectioners' sugar or cocoa before carefully removing the card.

Melting Chocolate

Melt chocolate slowly, as overheating will spoil both the flavor and texture. Dark chocolate should not be heated above 120°F; milk and white chocolate should not go above 110°F. Do not allow water or steam to come into contact with melting chocolate as this may cause it to stiffen. Leave chocolate uncovered after melting, as condensation could also cause it to stiffen.

Using a double boiler

1 Fill the bottom of a double boiler or saucepan about a quarter full. Fit the top pan or place a heatproof bowl over the saucepan. The water should not touch the top container. Bring the water to just below boiling point, then turn down the heat to the lowest possible setting.

2 Chop the chocolate or break it into squares and place in the top pan or bowl. Allow to melt completely. Stir until smooth. Keep the water at a very low simmer all the time.

▲ **Using the microwave** Chop the chocolate or break it into squares and place it in a bowl suitable for use in the microwave. Heat until just softened – chocolate burns easily in the microwave, so check often, remembering that chocolate retains its shape when melted in this way.

Approximate times for melting semisweet or milk chocolate in a 650–700 watt microwave oven are: 4 ounces, 2 minutes on High (100% power), 7–8 ounces 3 minutes on High (100% power), 4 ounces white chocolate, 2 minutes on Medium (50% power).

◀ **Using direct heat** This is only suitable for recipes where the chocolate is melted in plenty of other liquid, such as milk or cream. Chop the chocolate or break it into a saucepan. Add the liquid, then heat gently, stirring occasionally, until the chocolate has melted and the mixture is smooth.

Storing Cookies

Cookies should always be cooled completely before storing. When stored, crisp cookies tend to go soft, and soft ones can harden and dry out. The key to storing cookies is to choose an airtight container. This could be a jar or tin with a tight-fitting lid, or a rigid plastic box with a close-fitting lid. If you are not quite sure about the fit of a lid, put the cookies in a sealed plastic bag first. Alternatively, cover the top of the tin, jar or container with plastic wrap before putting on the lid.

▲ **Glass jars** Glass jars with airtight stoppers or corks, or screw-topped lids, allow the cookies to be seen. Found mostly in kitchen departments or shops, some jars come in wonderful shapes and colors.

▶ **Tins** Tins make excellent airtight containers for cookies and come in all shapes and sizes. Look for the more unconventional shapes and designs in large stores, kitchen shops and stationers.

Gift-wrapping Cookies

Cookies make wonderful gifts, and you can easily make the wrapping as special as the contents for an irresistible present.

▶ **Gift-wrapping materials** The emphasis on attractive gift-wrap has increased considerably in recent years. It is relatively simple to make small gifts at home and package them beautifully. Personalized gifts are as much a joy to give as to receive.

There are many shops that specialize in gift-wrapping materials. Papers, ribbons, different types of boxes, containers, labels and cards are all available. When making your own gifts, look out for unusual accessories with which to enhance the packaging of the fruits of your labors. Keep an eye open for innovative containers in second-hand, collectible and antique shops and flea markets.

▲ **Boxes** These make wonderful containers for cookies. You will find many different designs, colors and sizes in stationers, paper specialists or large stores. If your gift will be given and eaten quickly, a pretty box lined with tissue paper may be the answer.

▲ **Bags** Paper and fabric bags can be used for cookies that are given and eaten quickly. They come in a variety of sizes and often have a matching gift label attached. A utilitarian brown paper bag undergoes a complete transformation when it is spatter-sprayed with gold and silver paint. Here it is decorated with a trio of candies wired to the ribbon and with gilded hydrangea heads stuck onto one side.

▲ **Cellophane** For a simple yet stylish presentation, wrap neat piles of cookies in cellophane and tie with string or a pretty ribbon.

For a very special gift, choose a fine porcelain dish, cover with cellophane or clear wrap, and tie with a coordinating ribbon.

▲ Many different shapes and types of container make the gift seem that little bit extra special.

▶ **Gift cards and tags** These are often available to coordinate with your chosen paper, box or container. You can easily make your own tags by sticking your chosen paper onto a plain piece of card before making a hole in the corner and adding a ribbon. The choice of ribbons is overwhelming; even the simplest ribbons can transform a gift more than any other packaging.

Traditional
Cookies

Snickerdoodles, Tollhouse Cookies, Melting Moments, Ginger Cookies, Scottish Shortbread – these are not just cookies but an integral part of a country's national cuisine, even its national heritage. Such cookies are foods we have known, eaten and loved all our lives, so making them can easily result in a trip along memory lane.

Traditional cookies have been made by generations of family and country cooks, usually using local produce, as in Brittany Butter Cookies, which come from the rich dairy land of western France, and Oatmeal Wedges from Scotland. The ingredients are inexpensive, available, everyday items and the methods straightforward.

Cookies will usually keep well; if they lose their freshness or crispness, they can be refreshed in a low oven, set at about 325°F for approximately three minutes.

It is a good idea to make a large batch of cookie dough and keep some in the freezer, either as a ball of dough, or ready-shaped, depending on the amount of room available, so you can quickly cook some cookies when you need them. Cookies can also be frozen after baking, but after defrosting will need to be refreshed in a low oven before serving.

Granola Cookies

Makes 18

INGREDIENTS

½ cup butter or margarine
½ cup light brown sugar
⅓ cup crunchy peanut butter
1 egg
⅓ cup all-purpose flour
½ teaspoon baking powder
½ teaspoon ground cinnamon
pinch of salt
2 cups granola
⅓ cup raisins
½ cup walnuts, chopped

1 Preheat the oven to 350°F. Grease a baking sheet. Put the butter or margarine in a bowl.

2 With an electric mixer, cream the butter or margarine and sugar until light and fluffy. Beat in the peanut butter, then beat in the egg.

3 Sift the flour, baking powder, cinnamon and salt over the peanut butter mixture and stir to blend. Stir in the granola, raisins and walnuts. Taste the mixture to see if it needs more sugar, as granolas vary in sweetness.

4 Drop rounded tablespoonfuls of the batter onto the prepared baking sheet about 1 inch apart. Press gently with the back of a spoon to spread each mound into a circle.

5 Bake for about 15 minutes, until lightly colored. With a metal spatula, transfer to a wire rack and allow to cool.

Crunchy Oatmeal Cookies

Makes 14

INGREDIENTS

¼ cup butter or margarine
¼ cup sugar
1 egg yolk
1½ cups all-purpose flour
1 teaspoon baking soda
pinch of salt
½ cup rolled oats
½ cup crunchy nugget cereal

Variation For Nutty Oatmeal Cookies, substitute an equal quantity of chopped walnuts or pecans for the cereal, and prepare as described.

1 With an electric mixer, cream the butter or margarine and sugar together until light and fluffy. Mix in the egg yolk.

2 Sift over the flour, baking soda and salt, then stir into the butter mixture. Add the oats and cereal and stir to blend. Chill for at least 20 minutes.

3 Preheat the oven to 375°F. Grease a baking sheet. Flour the bottom of a glass.

4 Roll the dough into balls. Place them on the prepared baking sheet and flatten with the bottom of the glass.

5 Bake for 10–12 minutes, until golden. With a metal spatula, transfer to a wire rack to cool completely.

Coconut Oat Cookies

Makes 18

INGREDIENTS

2 cups quick-cooking oats
1 cup shredded coconut
1 cup butter or margarine, at
room temperature
$^1/_2$ cup granulated sugar
$^1/_4$ cup firmly packed dark brown
sugar
2 eggs
4 tablespoons milk
$1^1/_2$ teaspoons vanilla extract
1 cup all-purpose flour
$^1/_2$ teaspoon baking soda
pinch of salt
1 teaspoon ground cinnamon

1 Preheat the oven to 400°F. Lightly grease two baking sheets. Grease the bottom of a glass and dip in sugar.

2 Spread the oats and coconut on an ungreased baking sheet. Bake for 8–10 minutes, until golden brown, stirring occasionally.

3 With an electric mixer, cream the butter or margarine and both sugars until light and fluffy. Beat in the eggs, one at a time, then add the milk and vanilla extract. Sift over the dry ingredients and fold in. Stir in the oats and coconut.

4 Drop spoonfuls of the dough 1–2 inches apart on the baking sheets and flatten with the glass. Bake for 8–10 minutes. Transfer to a wire rack to cool.

Crunchy Jumbles

Makes 36

INGREDIENTS

$^1/_2$ cup butter or margarine, at
room temperature
1 cup sugar
1 egg
1 teaspoon vanilla extract
$1^1/_4$ cups all-purpose flour
$^1/_2$ teaspoon baking soda
pinch of salt
2 cups Rice Krispies
1 cup chocolate chips

Variation For even crunchier cookies, add $^1/_2$ cup walnuts, coarsely chopped, with the cereal and chocolate chips.

1 Preheat the oven to 350°F. Lightly grease two baking sheets.

2 With an electric mixer, cream the butter or margarine and sugar until light and fluffy. Beat in the egg and vanilla. Sift over the flour, baking soda and salt and fold in.

3 Add the cereal and chocolate chips. Stir to mix thoroughly.

4 Drop spoonfuls of the dough 1–2 inches apart on the prepared sheets. Bake for 10–12 minutes, until golden. Transfer to a wire rack to cool.

Malted Oat Crisps

These cookies are very crisp and crunchy – ideal to serve with morning coffee.

Makes 18

INGREDIENTS

1½ cups rolled oats
¼ cup packed light brown sugar
1 egg
4 tablespoons sunflower oil
2 tablespoons malt extract

1 Preheat the oven to 375°F. Lightly grease two baking sheets. Mix the rolled oats and brown sugar in a bowl, breaking up any lumps in the sugar. Add the egg, sunflower oil and malt extract, mix well, then let soak for 15 minutes.

2 Using a teaspoon, place small mounds of the mixture well apart on the prepared baking sheets. Press the mounds into 3-inch rounds with the back of a dampened fork.

3 Bake for 10–15 minutes, until golden brown. Allow to cool for 1 minute, then remove with a metal spatula and cool on a wire rack.

Variation To give these crisp cookies a fruity taste, add ½ cup chopped dates.

Shortbread

Makes 8

❧

INGREDIENTS

⅔ cup unsalted butter
⅓ cup sugar
1¼ cups all-purpose flour
⅓ cup rice flour
¼ teaspoon baking powder
pinch of salt

❧

1 Preheat the oven to 325°F. Grease a shallow 8 inch cake tin.

2 With an electric mixer, cream the butter and sugar together until light and fluffy. Sift over the flours, baking powder and salt and mix well.

3 Press the dough neatly into the prepared tin, smoothing the surface with the back of a spoon. Prick all over with a fork, then score into eight equal wedges.

4 Bake for 40–45 minutes. Leave in the tin until cool enough to handle, then unmold and recut the wedges while still hot.

Oatmeal Wedges

Makes 8

❧

INGREDIENTS

4 tablespoons butter
1½ tablespoons molasses
⅓ cup dark brown sugar
1¼ cups rolled oats
pinch of salt

❧

Variation If wished, add 1 teaspoon ground ginger to the melted butter.

1 Preheat the oven to 350°F. Line an 8 inch shallow cake tin with waxed paper and grease the paper.

2 Place the butter, molasses and sugar in a saucepan over a low heat. Cook, stirring, until melted and combined.

3 Remove from the heat and add the oats and salt. Stir to blend.

4 Spoon into the prepared cake tin and smooth the surface. Bake for 20–25 minutes until golden brown. Leave in the tin until cool enough to handle, then unmold and cut into eight equal wedges while still hot.

Melting Moments

These cookies are very crisp and light – and they melt in your mouth.

Makes 16–20

❦

INGREDIENTS

*3 tablespoons butter or margarine
5 tablespoons lard or
vegetable shortening
¹/₂ cup sugar
¹/₂ egg, beaten
few drops of vanilla or
almond extract
1¹/₄ cups self-rising flour
rolled oats for coating
4–5 candied cherries, quartered*

❦

1 Preheat the oven to 350°F. Grease two baking sheets. Cream together the butter or margarine, lard and sugar, then gradually beat in the egg and vanilla or almond extract.

2 Stir the flour into the beaten mixture, then roll into 16–20 small balls in your hands.

3 Spread the rolled oats on a sheet of waxed paper and toss the balls in them to coat evenly.

4 Place the balls, spaced slightly apart, on the prepared baking sheets, place a piece of cherry on top of each and bake for 15–20 minutes, until lightly browned. Allow the cookies to cool for a few minutes before transferring to a wire rack.

Apricot Yogurt Cookies

These soft cookies are very quick to make and are useful for lunch boxes.

Makes 16

INGREDIENTS

1½ cups all-purpose flour
1 teaspoon baking powder
1 teaspoon ground cinnamon
1 cup rolled oats
½ cup light brown sugar, plus
some for sprinkling
¾ cup chopped ready-to-eat dried
apricots
1 tablespoon slivered hazelnuts
or almonds
⅔ cup plain yogurt
3 tablespoons sunflower oil

1 Preheat the oven to 375°F. Lightly oil a large baking sheet.

2 Sift together the flour, baking powder and cinnamon. Stir in the oats, sugar, apricots and nuts.

Cook's Tip These cookies do not keep well, so it is best to eat them within two days, or to freeze them. Pack into polythene bags and freeze for up to four months.

3 Beat together the yogurt and oil, then stir evenly into the flour mixture to make a firm dough. If necessary, add a little more yogurt. Use your hands to roll the mixture into about 16 small balls.

4 Place the balls on the prepared baking sheet and flatten with a fork. Sprinkle with light brown sugar. Bake for 15–20 minutes, until firm and golden brown. Transfer to a wire rack and leave to cool.

Applesauce Cookies

These fruit-flavored cookies are a favorite with children.

Makes 36

INGREDIENTS

*1 pound cooking apples, peeled,
cored and chopped
3 tablespoons water
$\frac{1}{2}$ cup sugar
$\frac{1}{2}$ cup butter or margarine
1 cup all-purpose flour
$\frac{1}{2}$ teaspoon baking powder
$\frac{1}{4}$ teaspoon baking soda
pinch of salt
$\frac{1}{2}$ teaspoon ground cinnamon
$\frac{1}{2}$ cup chopped walnuts*

1 Cook the apples with the water in a covered saucepan over low heat until the apple is tender. Cool slightly, then purée in a blender or mash with a fork. Measure out $\frac{1}{4}$ cup.

2 Preheat the oven to 375°F. Grease a baking sheet. In a medium-sized bowl, cream together the sugar and butter or margarine until well mixed. Beat in the applesauce.

Cook's Tip If the applesauce is too runny, put it in a strainer over a bowl and let it drain for 10 minutes before measuring it out.

3 Sift the flour, baking powder, baking soda, salt and cinnamon into the mixture, and stir to blend. Fold in the chopped walnuts.

4 Drop teaspoonfuls of the dough onto the prepared baking sheet, spacing them about 2 inches apart.

5 Bake the cookies for 8–10 minutes, until they are golden brown. Transfer to a wire rack and allow to cool.

Chocolate Chip Hazelnut Cookies

Chocolate chip cookies, with a delicious nutty flavor.

Makes 36

❦

INGREDIENTS

1 cup all-purpose flour
1 teaspoon baking powder
pinch of salt
¹/₃ cup butter or margarine
1¹/₂ cups granulated sugar
¹/₃ cup light brown sugar
1 egg
1 teaspoon vanilla extract
²/₃ cup chocolate chips
¹/₂ cup hazelnuts, chopped

❦

3 Stir in the chocolate chips and half of the hazelnuts, using a wooden spoon.

4 Drop teaspoonfuls of the mixture onto the prepared baking sheets, to form ¹/₄ inch mounds. Space the cookies 1–2 inches apart.

5 Flatten each cookie lightly with a wet fork. Sprinkle the remaining hazelnuts on top of the cookies and press lightly into the surface.

6 Bake for 10–12 minutes until golden. Transfer the biscuits to a wire rack and leave to cool.

1 Preheat the oven to 350°F. Grease 2–3 baking sheets. Sift the flour, baking powder and salt into a small bowl. Set aside.

2 With an electric mixer, cream together the butter or margarine and the sugars. Beat in the egg and vanilla extract. Add the flour mixture and beat well with the mixer on low speed.

Peanut Butter Cookies

For extra crunch, add ¹/₂ cup chopped peanuts with the peanut butter.

Makes 24

INGREDIENTS

1 cup all-purpose flour
¹/₂ teaspoon baking soda
pinch of salt
¹/₂ cup butter
¹/₄ cup firmly packed light brown sugar
1 egg
1 teaspoon vanilla extract
1 cup crunchy peanut butter

1 Sift together the flour, baking soda and salt and set aside.

2 With an electric mixer, cream together the butter and sugar until light and fluffy.

3 In another bowl, mix the egg and vanilla extract, then gradually beat into the butter mixture.

4 Stir in the peanut butter and blend thoroughly. Stir in the dry ingredients. Chill for at least 30 minutes, until firm.

5 Preheat the oven to 350°F. Grease two baking sheets.

6 Spoon out rounded teaspoonfuls of the dough and roll into balls.

7 Place the balls on the prepared baking sheets and press flat with a fork into circles about 2¹/₂ inches in diameter, making a criss-cross pattern. Bake for 12–15 minutes, until lightly colored. Transfer to a wire rack to cool.

Tollhouse Cookies

Makes 24

INGREDIENTS

¹/₂ cup butter or margarine
¹/₄ cup granulated sugar
¹/₂ cup firmly packed dark brown sugar
1 egg
¹/₂ teaspoon vanilla extract
1¹/₈ cups all-purpose flour
¹/₂ teaspoon baking soda
pinch of salt
1 cup chocolate chips
¹/₂ cup walnuts, chopped

1 Preheat the oven to 350°F. Grease two baking sheets.

2 With an electric mixer, cream together the butter or margarine and the two sugars until the mixture is light and fluffy.

3 In another bowl, mix the egg and vanilla extract, then gradually beat into the butter mixture. Sift over the flour, baking soda and salt. Stir to blend.

4 Add the chocolate chips and walnuts, and mix to combine thoroughly.

5 Place heaping teaspoonfuls of the dough 2 inches apart on the prepared baking sheets. Bake for 10–15 minutes, until lightly colored. With a metal spatula, transfer to a wire rack to cool.

Snickerdoodles

Makes 30

INGREDIENTS

¹/₂ cup butter
1¹/₂ cups sugar
1 teaspoon vanilla extract
2 eggs
¹/₄ cup milk
3¹/₂ cups all-purpose flour
1 teaspoon baking soda
¹/₂ cup walnuts or pecans, finely
chopped
For the coating
5 tablespoons sugar
2 tablespoons ground cinnamon

1 With an electric mixer, beat the butter until light and creamy. Add the sugar and vanilla extract and continue until fluffy. Beat in the eggs, then the milk.

2 Sift the flour and baking soda over the butter mixture and stir to blend. Stir in the nuts. Refrigerate for 15 minutes. Preheat the oven to 375°F. Grease two baking sheets.

3 To make the coating, mix the sugar and cinnamon. Roll tablespoonfuls of the dough into walnut-size balls. Roll the balls in the sugar mixture. You may need to work in batches.

4 Place the balls 2 inches apart on the prepared baking sheets and flatten slightly. Bake for about 10 minutes, until golden. Transfer to a wire rack to cool.

Chewy Chocolate Cookies

Makes 18

INGREDIENTS

4 egg whites
2¹/₂ cups confectioners' sugar
1 cup cocoa powder
2 tablespoons all-purpose flour
1 teaspoon instant coffee powder
1 tablespoon water
1 cup walnuts, finely chopped

1 Preheat the oven to 350°F. Line two baking sheets with waxed paper and then grease the paper well.

2 With an electric mixer, beat the egg whites until frothy.

3 Sift the sugar, cocoa, flour and coffee into the whites. Add the water and continue beating on low speed to blend, then on high for a few minutes, until the mixture thickens. With a rubber spatula, fold in the walnuts.

4 Place generous spoonfuls of the mixture 1 inch apart on the prepared baking sheets. Bake for 12–15 minutes, until firm and cracked on top but soft on the inside. With a metal spatula, transfer to a wire rack to cool.

Variation Add ¹/₂ cup chocolate chips to the dough with the chopped walnuts.

Buttermilk Cookies

Makes 15

❦

INGREDIENTS

1¹/₂ cups all-purpose flour
pinch of salt
1 teaspoon baking powder
¹/₂ teaspoon baking soda
4 tablespoons cold butter or
margarine
³/₄ cup buttermilk

❦

1 Preheat the oven to 425°F. Grease a baking sheet.

2 Sift the dry ingredients into a bowl. Rub in the butter or margarine until the mixture resembles coarse crumbs.

3 Gradually pour in the buttermilk, stirring with a fork until the mixture forms a soft dough.

4 Roll out to about ¹/₂ inch thick. Stamp out 2-inch circles with a cookie cutter.

5 Place on the prepared baking sheet and bake for 12–15 minutes, until golden. Serve warm or at room temperature.

Shortcake Cookies

These make a simple accompaniment to meals, or a snack with fruit preserves.

Makes 8

❦

INGREDIENTS

1¹/₃ cups all-purpose flour
2 tablespoons sugar
1 tablespoon baking powder
pinch of salt
5 tablespoons cold butter, chopped
¹/₂ cup milk

❦

Variation For Berry Shortcake, split the cookies in half while still warm. Butter one half, top with lightly sugared fresh berries, such as strawberries, raspberries or blueberries, and sandwich with the other half. Serve with dollops of whipped cream.

1 Preheat the oven to 425°F. Grease a baking sheet. Sift the flour, sugar, baking powder and salt into a bowl.

2 Rub in the butter until the mixture resembles coarse crumbs. Pour in the milk and stir with a fork to form a soft dough.

3 Roll out the dough to about ¹/₄ inch thick. Stamp out circles with a 2¹/₂-inch cookie cutter.

4 Place on the prepared baking sheet and bake for about 12 minutes, until golden. Serve these soft cookies hot or warm, spread with butter for meals. To accompany tea or coffee, serve with butter and jam or honey.

Traditional Sugar Cookies

Makes 36

❧

INGREDIENTS

*3 cups all-purpose flour
1 teaspoon baking soda
2 teaspoons baking powder
¹/₂ teaspoon grated nutmeg
¹/₂ cup butter or margarine
1 cup sugar
¹/₂ teaspoon vanilla extract
1 egg
¹/₂ cup milk
colored or raw sugar for
sprinkling*

❧

1 Sift the flour, baking soda, baking powder and nutmeg into a small bowl. Set aside.

2 With an electric mixer, cream together the butter or margarine, granulated sugar and vanilla extract until the mixture is light and fluffy. Add the egg and beat to mix well.

3 Add the flour mixture alternately with the milk to make a soft dough. Wrap in plastic wrap and chill for at least 30 minutes.

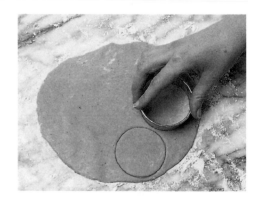

4 Preheat the oven to 350°F. Roll out the dough on a lightly floured surface to ¹/₈ inch thick. Cut into rounds or other shapes with floured cookie cutters.

5 Transfer to ungreased baking sheets. Sprinkle with colored or raw sugar. Bake for 10–12 minutes, until golden brown. Transfer the cookies to a wire rack to cool.

Brittany Butter Cookies

These little biscuits are similar to shortbread, but richer. Traditionally, they are made with lightly salted butter.

Makes 18–20

INGREDIENTS

6 egg yolks, lightly beaten
1 tablespoon milk
2¼ cups all-purpose flour
¾ cup sugar
scant 1 cup butter

1 Preheat the oven to 350°F. Butter a heavy baking sheet. Mix 1 tablespoon of the egg yolks with the milk to make a glaze.

2 Sift the flour into a bowl. Add the egg yolks, sugar and butter, and work them together until creamy.

3 Gradually bring in a little flour at a time until it forms a slightly sticky dough.

4 Using floured hands, pat out the dough to about ¼ inch thick and cut out rounds using a 3 inch cutter. Transfer the rounds to the prepared baking sheet, brush each with a little egg glaze, then, using the back of a knife, score with lines to create a lattice pattern.

5 Bake for about 12–15 minutes, until golden. Cool on the baking sheet on a wire rack for 15 minutes, then carefully remove the biscuits and leave to cool completely on the rack.

Cook's Tip To make a large Brittany Butter Cake, pat the dough with well-floured hands into a 9 inch loose-based cake pan or springform pan. Brush with egg glaze and score the lattice pattern on top. Bake for 45 minutes–1 hour, until firm to the touch and golden brown.

Toffee Cookies

Makes 36

INGREDIENTS

³/₄ cup unsalted butter, melted
1³/₄ cups instant oatmeal
¹/₂ cup packed light brown sugar
¹/₂ cup dark corn syrup
2 tablespoons vanilla extract
large pinch of salt
³/₄ cup semisweet chocolate, grated
¹/₃ cup chopped walnuts

1 Preheat the oven to 400°F. Grease a 15 x 10-inch baking pan.

2 Mix together the butter, oats, sugar, syrup, vanilla extract and salt and press into the prepared pan. Bake for about 15–18 minutes, until the mixture is brown and bubbly.

3 Remove from the oven and immediately sprinkle on the chocolate. Set aside for 10 minutes, then spread the chocolate over the base. Sprinkle on the nuts. Transfer to a wire rack to cool. Cut into squares.

Rose Water Thins

These light, crunchy cookies are easy to make and bake in minutes.

Makes 60

INGREDIENTS

1 cup lightly salted butter
1 cup sugar, plus extra
for sprinkling
1 egg
1 tablespoon light cream
2¹/₂ cups all-purpose flour
pinch of salt
1 teaspoon baking powder
1 tablespoon rose water

1 Preheat the oven to 375°F. Line two baking sheets with baking parchment.

2 Soften the butter and mix with all the other ingredients until you have a firm dough. Mold the mixture into an even roll and wrap in waxed paper. Chill until it is firm enough to slice very thinly. This will take 1–1¹/₂ hours.

3 Arrange the cookies on the prepared baking sheets with enough space for them to spread. Sprinkle with a little sugar and bake for about 10 minutes, until they are just turning brown at the edges.

Scottish Shortbread

Light, ~~crumbly~~ *looks very professional when shaped in a mold,* ~~y~~*ou could also shape it by hand.*

M~~~~
8 indiv~~~~

INGR~~~~
⅓ cup all-p~~~~
½ cup cor~~~~
¼ cup sugar, plu~~~~
sprinkling~~~~
½ cup unsalted butter~~~~

1 Preheat the oven to 325°F. Lightly flour the mold and line a baking sheet with baking parchment. Sift the flour, cornstarch and sugar into a mixing bowl. Rub the butter into the flour mixture until it binds together and you can knead it into a soft dough.

2 Place the dough into the mold and press to fit neatly. Invert the mold onto the baking sheet and tap firmly to release the dough shape. Bake for 35–40 minutes, until pale golden in color.

3 Sprinkle the top of the shortbread with a little sugar and cool on the baking sheet. Wrap in cellophane paper or place in a box tied with ribbon to make a delicious Christmas gift.

Spanish Churros

Makes 24

INGREDIENTS

1 cup water
1 tablespoon sugar, plus extra for coating
pinch of salt
1¹/₂ cups all-purpose flour
1 egg
oil for deep frying
¹/₂ lime or lemon

Cook's Tip A funnel can be used to shape the churros. Close the end with a finger, add the batter, then release into the oil in small columns.

1 Bring the water, sugar and salt to a boil. Remove from the heat and beat in the flour until smooth.

2 Beat in the egg, using a wooden spoon, until the mixture is smooth and satiny. Set the batter aside.

3 Pour the oil into a deep frying pan to a depth of about 2 inches. Add the lime or lemon, then heat the oil to 375°F, until a cube of day old bread added to the oil browns in 30–60 seconds.

4 Pour the batter into a pastry bag fitted with a fluted nozzle. Pipe 3-inch strips of batter and then add to the oil, a few at a time. Fry for 3–4 minutes, until golden brown.

5 Using a slotted spoon, remove the churros from the pan and drain on paper towels. Roll the hot churros in sugar before serving with a cup of thick hot chocolate.

Golden Pillows

Makes 30

INGREDIENTS

2 cups all-purpose flour, sifted
1 tablespoon baking powder
pinch of salt
2 tablespoons lard, margarine or vegetable shortening
³/₄ cup water
corn oil for frying
syrup or honey, to serve

Cook's Tip Use your imagination when deciding what to serve with the pillows. Sprinkle them with cinnamon and sugar, or syrup flavored with rum.

1 Put the flour, baking powder and salt into a large bowl. Lightly rub in the lard or margarine, using your fingertips, until the mixture resembles coarse breadcrumbs.

2 Gradually stir in the water, using a fork, until the mixture clings together to form a soft dough.

3 Shape the dough into a ball, then turn onto a lightly floured surface and knead very gently until smooth. Roll out thinly to a rectangle measuring about 18 x 15 inches. Using a sharp knife, carefully cut about thirty 3-inch squares. For a decorative edge, use a pastry wheel to cut out the squares.

4 Heat the oil to 375°F, until a cube of day old bread browns in 30–60 seconds.

5 Fry the squares, a few at a time, in the oil. As they brown and puff up, turn over to cook the other side. Remove with a slotted spoon and drain on paper towels. It is important that the temperature of the oil remains constant during the cooking process. Serve warm, with syrup or honey.

Chunky Chocolate Drops

Do not allow these cookies to cool completely on the baking sheet or they will become too crisp and will break when you try to lift them.

Makes 18

❦

INGREDIENTS

6 ounces semisweet chocolate, chopped
¹/₂ cup unsalted butter, chopped
2 eggs
¹/₂ cup granulated sugar
¹/₃ cup light brown sugar
¹/₃ cup all-purpose flour
¹/₄ cup cocoa powder
1 teaspoon baking powder
2 teaspoons vanilla extract
pinch of salt
1 cup pecans, toasted and coarsely chopped
1 cup semisweet chocolate chips
4 ounces good-quality white chocolate, chopped into ¹/₄-inch pieces
¹/₂ cup good-quality milk chocolate, chopped into ¹/₄-inch pieces

❦

1 Preheat the oven to 325°F. Grease two large baking sheets. In a medium saucepan over low heat, melt the semisweet chocolate and butter, stirring until smooth. Remove from the heat and set aside to cool slightly.

2 In a large mixing bowl, using an electric mixer, beat the eggs and sugars for 2–3 minutes, until pale and creamy. Gradually pour in the melted chocolate mixture, beating until well blended. Beat in the flour, cocoa powder, baking powder, vanilla extract and salt until just blended. Stir in the nuts, chocolate chips and white and milk chocolate pieces.

3 Drop heaping tablespoons of the mixture onto the prepared baking sheets 4 inches apart. Flatten each to 3-inch rounds. Bake for 8–10 minutes, until the tops are shiny and cracked and the edges look crisp; do not overbake or the cookies will become fragile.

4 Remove the baking sheets to a wire rack to cool for 2 minutes, then transfer cookies to the rack to cool.

Chocolate Marzipan Cookies

These crisp little cookies satisfy a sweet tooth and have a little almond surprise inside.

Makes 36

❦

INGREDIENTS

scant 1 cup unsalted butter
generous 1 cup light brown sugar
1 egg
2¹/₂ cups all-purpose flour
4 tablespoons cocoa powder
7 ounces white almond paste
4 ounces white chocolate, chopped

❦

1 Preheat the oven to 375°F. Lightly grease two large baking sheets. Cream the butter with the sugar in a bowl until pale and fluffy. Add the egg and beat well.

2 Sift the flour and cocoa over the mixture. Stir in, first with a wooden spoon, then with clean hands, pressing the mixture together to make a fairly soft dough.

Cook's Tip If the dough is too sticky to roll, chill it for about 30 minutes, then try again.

3 Roll out about half the dough on a lightly floured surface to a thickness of about ¹/₄ inch. Using a 2 inch cookie cutter, cut out rounds, re-rolling the dough as required until you have about 36 rounds.

4 Cut the almond paste into about 36 equal pieces. Roll into balls, flatten slightly and place one on each round of dough. Roll out the remaining dough, cut out more rounds, then place on top of the almond paste. Press the dough edges to seal. Bake for 10–12 minutes until the cookies have risen well. Cool completely. Melt the white chocolate, spoon into a paper piping bag and pipe onto the biscuits.

Double Chocolate Cookies

Keep these luscious treats under lock and key unless you're feeling generous.

Makes 18–20

❧

INGREDIENTS

½ cup unsalted butter
⅔ cup firmly packed light brown sugar
1 egg
1 teaspoon vanilla extract
1¼ cups self-rising flour
¾ cup rolled oats
4 ounces semisweet chocolate, coarsely chopped
4 ounces white chocolate, coarsely chopped

❧

Cook's Tip If you're short of time when making the cookies, substitute chocolate chips for the chopped chocolate. Chopped crystallized ginger would make a delicious addition as well.

1 Preheat the oven to 375°F. Lightly grease two baking sheets. Cream the butter with the sugar in a bowl until pale and fluffy. Add the egg and vanilla extract and beat well.

2 Sift the flour over the mixture and fold in lightly with a metal spoon, then add the oats and chopped semisweet and white chocolate and stir until evenly mixed.

3 Place small spoonfuls of the mixture in 18–20 rocky mounds on the prepared baking sheets, leaving space for spreading.

4 Bake for 15–20 minutes, until beginning to turn pale golden. Cool for 2–3 minutes on the baking sheets, then transfer to wire racks to cool completely.

Chocolate and Nut Refrigerator Cookies

The dough must be chilled thoroughly before it can be sliced and baked.

Makes 50

INGREDIENTS

2 cups all-purpose flour
pinch of salt
2 ounces semisweet chocolate,
chopped
1 cup unsalted butter
1 cup sugar
2 eggs
1 teaspoon vanilla extract
1 cup walnuts, finely chopped

Variation For two-tone cookies, melt only 1 ounce chocolate. Combine all the ingredients, except the chocolate, as above. Divide the dough in half. Add the chocolate to one half. Roll out the plain dough on to a flat sheet. Roll out the chocolate dough, place on top of the plain dough and roll up. Wrap, slice and bake as described.

2 With an electric mixer, cream the butter until soft. Add the sugar and continue beating until the mixture is light and fluffy.

3 Mix the eggs with the vanilla extract, then gradually stir into the butter mixture.

4 Stir in the chocolate, then the flour followed by the nuts.

5 Divide the dough into four parts, and roll each into 2 inch diameter logs. Wrap tightly in foil and chill or freeze until firm.

6 Preheat the oven to 375°F. Grease two baking sheets. Cut the dough into ¼ inch slices. Place on the prepared sheets and bake for about 10 minutes. Transfer to wire racks to cool.

1 In a small bowl, sift together the flour and salt. Set aside. Melt the chocolate in the top of a double boiler, or in a heatproof bowl set over a saucepan of hot water. Set aside.

Chocolate Kisses

These rich little cookies look attractive mixed together on a plate and dusted with confectioners' sugar. Serve them with ice cream or simply with coffee.

Makes 24

❧

INGREDIENTS

3 ounces semisweet chocolate, chopped
3 ounces white chocolate, chopped
¹/₂ cup butter
¹/₂ cup granulated sugar
2 eggs
2 cups all-purpose flour
confectioners' sugar, to decorate

❧

1 Put each chocolate into a small bowl and melt it over a saucepan of hot, but not boiling, water, stirring until smooth. Set aside to cool.

2 Beat together the butter and granulated sugar until pale and fluffy. Beat in the eggs, one at a time.

3 Sift the flour over the butter, sugar and egg mixture and mix in thoroughly.

4 Halve the mixture and divide it between the two bowls of chocolate. Mix each chocolate in well. Knead the doughs until smooth, wrap them in plastic wrap and chill for 1 hour. Preheat the oven to 375°F. Grease two baking sheets.

5 Shape slightly rounded teaspoonfuls of both doughs roughly into balls. Roll the balls in the palms of your hands to make neater ball shapes. Arrange the balls on the prepared baking sheets and bake for 10–12 minutes. Dust with sifted confectioners' sugar and then transfer to a wire rack to cool.

Chocolate Pretzels

Makes 28

❦

INGREDIENTS

1 cup all-purpose flour
pinch of salt
3 tablespoons cocoa powder
¹/₂ cup butter
²/₃ cup sugar
1 egg
1 egg white, lightly beaten, for
glazing
sugar crystals for sprinkling

❦

1 Sift together the flour, salt and cocoa powder. Set aside. Grease two baking sheets.

2 With an electric mixer, cream the butter until light. Add the sugar and continue beating until light and fluffy. Beat in the egg. Add the dry ingredients and stir to blend. Gather the dough into a ball, wrap in waxed paper, and chill for 1 hour, or freeze for 30 minutes.

3 Roll the dough into 28 small balls. If the dough is sticky, flour your hands. Chill the balls until needed. Preheat the oven to 375°F.

4 Roll each ball into a rope about 10 inches long. With each rope, form a loop with the two ends facing you. Twist the ends and fold back on to the circle, pressing in to make a pretzel shape. Place on the prepared baking sheets.

5 Brush the pretzels with the egg white. Sprinkle sugar crystals over the tops and bake for 10–12 minutes until firm. Transfer to a wire rack to cool.

59

Chocolate, Maple and Walnut Swirls

Makes 12

❧

INGREDIENTS

4 cups all-purpose flour
¹/₂ teaspoon ground cinnamon
4 tablespoons unsalted butter, chopped
¹/₄ cup granulated sugar
1 envelope easy-blend active dry yeast
1 egg yolk
¹/₂ cup water
4 tablespoons milk
3 tablespoons maple syrup, to finish
For the filling
3 tablespoons unsalted butter, melted
¹/₄ packed cup light brown sugar
1 cup semisweet chocolate chips
³/₄ cup chopped walnuts

❧

1 Grease a deep 9-inch springform cake pan. Sift the flour and cinnamon into a bowl, then rub in the butter until the mixture resembles coarse bread crumbs.

2 Stir in the sugar and yeast. In a cup, beat the egg yolk, with the water and milk, then stir into the dry ingredients to make a soft dough.

3 Knead until smooth, then roll out to about 16 x 12 inches. Brush with melted butter.

4 To make the filling, sprinkle the dough with the brown sugar, chocolate chips and chopped walnuts.

5 Roll up the dough from a long side like a jelly roll, then cut into 12 thick, even-sized slices.

6 Pack the slices closely together in the prepared cake pan. Cover and leave in a warm place for 1¹/₂ hours, until well risen and springy to the touch. Preheat the oven to 425°F.

7 Bake for 30–35 minutes, until well risen, golden brown and firm. Remove from the pan and transfer to a wire rack. To finish, spoon the maple syrup over the cake. Pull the pieces apart to serve.

Cook's Tip The amount of liquid added to the dry ingredients may have to be adjusted slightly as some flours absorb more liquid than others.

Old-fashioned Ginger Cookies

Makes 60

❧

INGREDIENTS

2¹/₂ cups all-purpose flour
1 teaspoon baking soda
1¹/₂ teaspoons ground ginger
¹/₄ teaspoon ground cinnamon
¹/₄ teaspoon ground cloves
¹/₂ cup butter or margarine
1¹/₂ cups sugar
1 egg, beaten
4 tablespoons black molasses
1 teaspoon fresh lemon juice

❧

1 Preheat the oven to 325°F. Grease 3–4 baking trays.

2 Sift the flour, baking soda and spices into a small bowl. Set aside.

3 With an electric mixer, cream together the butter or margarine and two-thirds of the sugar.

4 Stir in the egg, molasses and lemon juice. Add the flour mixture and mix in thoroughly with a wooden spoon to make a soft dough.

5 Shape the dough into ³/₄ inch balls. Roll the balls in the remaining sugar and place them about 2 inches apart on the prepared baking trays.

6 Bake for about 12 minutes, until the biscuits are just firm to the touch. With a slotted spatula, transfer the biscuits to a wire rack and leave to cool.

Double Gingerbread Cookies

Packed in little bags or into a gingerbread box, these pretty cookies would make a lovely gift.

They are easy to make, but will have everyone wondering how you did it!

Makes 25

INGREDIENTS

For the golden gingerbread
mixture
1¹/₂ cups all-purpose flour
¹/₄ teaspoon baking soda
pinch of salt
1 teaspoon ground cinnamon
¹/₃ cup unsalted butter, chopped
¹/₃ cup sugar
2 tablespoons maple or light
corn syrup
1 egg, beaten
For the chocolate gingerbread
mixture
1¹/₂ cups all-purpose flour
pinch of salt
2 teaspoons ground pumpkin
pie spice
¹/₂ teaspoon baking soda
4 tablespoons cocoa powder
¹/₃ cup unsalted butter, chopped
¹/₃ cup firmly packed light
brown sugar
1 egg, beaten

1 To make the golden gingerbread,
sift together the flour, baking
soda, salt and spices. Rub the butter
into the flour in a large bowl, until
the mixture resembles fine
breadcrumbs. Add the sugar, syrup
and egg yolk and mix to a firm
dough. Knead lightly. Wrap in plastic
wrap and chill for 30 minutes
before shaping.

2 To make the chocolate
gingerbread, sift together the
flour, salt, spice, baking soda and
Knead the butter into the flour in a
large bowl. Add the sugar and egg and
mix to a firm dough. Knead lightly.
Wrap in plastic wrap and chill for at
least 30 minutes.

3 Roll out half of the chocolate
dough on a floured surface to an
11 x 1¹/₂-inch rectangle, ¹/₂ inch thick.
Repeat with half the golden
gingerbread dough. Using a knife, cut
both lengths into seven long, thin
strips. Lay the strips together, side by
side, alternating the colors.

4 Roll out the remaining golden
gingerbread dough with your
hands into a long sausage, ³/₄-inch
wide and the length of the strips. Lay
the sausage of dough down the center
of the striped dough.

5 Carefully bring the striped dough
up around the sausage and press
it gently into position to enclose the
sausage completely. Roll the
remaining chocolate dough into a
thin rectangle measuring
approximately 11 x 5 inches.

6 Bring the chocolate dough up
around the striped dough, to
enclose it. Press gently into place.
Wrap and chill for 30 minutes.

7 Preheat the oven to 350°F. Grease
a large baking sheet. Cut the
gingerbread roll into thin slices and
place them, slightly apart, on the
prepared baking sheet.

8 Bake for about 12–15 minutes,
until just beginning to color
around the edges. Leave on the
baking sheet for 3 minutes and
transfer to a wire rack to cool
completely.

Spicy Pepper Cookies

Makes 48

INGREDIENTS

1¾ cups all-purpose flour
½ cup cornstarch
2 teaspoons baking powder
½ teaspoon ground cardamom
½ teaspoon ground cinnamon
½ teaspoon grated nutmeg
½ teaspoon ground ginger
½ teaspoon ground allspice
pinch of salt
½ teaspoon freshly ground black pepper
1 cup butter or margarine
1⅓ cups light brown sugar
½ teaspoon vanilla extract
1 teaspoon finely grated lemon rind
¼ cup whipping cream
¾ cup finely ground almonds
2 tablespoons confectioners' sugar

1 Preheat the oven to 350°F.

2 Sift the flour, cornstarch, baking powder, spices, salt and pepper into a bowl. Set aside.

3 With an electric mixer, cream the butter or margarine and brown sugar together until light and fluffy. Beat in the vanilla extract and grated lemon rind.

4 With the mixer on low speed, add the flour mixture alternately with the whipping cream, beginning and ending with flour. Stir in the ground almonds.

5 Shape the dough into ¾-inch balls. Place them on ungreased baking sheets, about 1 inch apart. Bake for 15–20 minutes, until golden brown underneath.

6 Allow to cool on the baking sheets for about 1 minute before transferring to a wire rack to cool completely. Before serving, sprinkle lightly with confectioners' sugar.

Lavender Heart Cookies

*In folklore, lavender has always been linked with love, as has food, so make some heart-
shaped cookies and serve them on Valentine's Day or any other romantic anniversary.*

Makes 16–18

❦

INGREDIENTS

½ cup unsalted butter
¼ cup granulated sugar
1½ cups all-purpose flour
2 tablespoons fresh lavender
florets or 1 tablespoon dried
culinary lavender, roughly
chopped
2 tablespoons superfine sugar for
sprinkling

❦

1 Cream together the butter and
sugar until fluffy. Stir in the flour
and lavender and bring the mixture
together in a soft ball. Cover and chill
for 15 minutes.

2 Preheat the oven to 400°F. Roll
out the dough on a lightly
floured surface and stamp out about
18 cookies using a 2 inch heart-
shaped cutter. Place on a heavy
baking sheet and bake for about
10 minutes, until golden.

3 Sprinkle with sugar then leave
the cookies standing for 5 minutes
to set. Using a metal spatula, transfer
carefully from the baking sheet onto
a wire rack to cool completely. The
cookies can be stored in an airtight
container for up to one week.

Vanilla Crescents

These attractively shaped cookies are sweet and delicate, ideal for an elegant afternoon tea.

Makes 36

❧

INGREDIENTS

1¼ cups unblanched almonds
1 cup all-purpose flour
pinch of salt
1 cup unsalted butter
½ cup granulated sugar
1 teaspoon vanilla extract
confectioners' sugar for dusting

❧

1 Grind the almonds with a few tablespoons of the flour in a food processor, blender or nut grinder.

2 Sift the remaining flour with the salt into a bowl. Set aside.

3 With an electric mixer, cream together the butter and sugar until light and fluffy.

4 Add the almonds, vanilla extract and the flour mixture. Stir to mix well. Gather the dough into a ball, wrap in waxed paper, and chill for at least 30 minutes.

5 Preheat the oven to 325°F. Lightly grease two baking sheets.

6 Break off walnut-size pieces of dough and roll into small cylinders about ½ inch in diameter. Bend into small crescents and place on the prepared baking sheets.

7 Bake for about 20 minutes, until dry but not brown. Transfer to a wire rack to cool only slightly. Set the rack over a baking sheet and dust with an even layer of confectioners' sugar. Allow to cool completely.

Mexican Aniseed Cookies

Makes 24

❧

INGREDIENTS

1½ cups all-purpose flour
1 teaspoon baking powder
pinch of salt
½ cup unsalted butter
½ cup sugar
1 egg
1 teaspoon whole aniseed
1 tablespoon brandy
¼ cup sugar mixed with
½ teaspoon ground cinnamon
for sprinkling

❧

1 Sift together the flour, baking powder and salt. Set aside.

2 Beat the butter with the sugar until soft and fluffy. Add the egg, aniseed and brandy and beat until incorporated. Fold in the dry ingredients until just blended to a dough. Chill for 30 minutes.

3 Preheat the oven to 350°F. Grease two baking sheets.

4 On a lightly floured surface, roll out the chilled dough to about ⅛ inch thick.

5 With a floured cutter, pastry wheel or knife, cut out the cookies into squares, diamonds or other shapes. The traditional shape for biscochitos is a fleur-de-lis but you might find this a bit too ambitious.

6 Place on the prepared baking sheets and sprinkle lightly with the cinnamon sugar.

7 Bake for about 10 minutes, until just barely golden. Cool on the baking sheet for 5 minutes before transferring to a wire rack to cool completely. The cookies can be kept in an airtight container for up to one week.

Festive and Fancy Cookies

Over the years, some cookies have become associated with certain festivals – Jeweled Christmas Trees dangle enticingly from the tree at Christmas, Easter Cookies always find their way into the cookie jar at that time of the year, and at carnival time Italians would feel deprived if Italian Pastry Twists did not make an appearance. Other cookies are festive just because they are fancy. Chocolate-Dipped Hazelnut Crescents or Black-and-White Ginger Florentines immediately perk up the spirits and make you feel something special is happening.

If you are making cookies for a holiday period such as school holidays, try to select recipes that keep well so you can make them a week or so in advance. Alternatively, freeze them, either raw or baked. Don't forget to make a note of how long they need to thaw, plus the baking time for raw cookies, and remember that cooked ones will benefit from being refreshed in the oven.

Baklava

This, the queen of all pastries, is enjoyed all year but is specially associated with many Greek holidays and festivities.

Makes 30

INGREDIENTS

3 cups ground pistachios
1¼ cups confectioners' sugar
1 tablespoon ground cardamom
⅔ cup unsalted butter, melted
1 pound filo pastry, defrosted
For the syrup
2 cups granulated sugar
1¼ cups water
2 tablespoons rose water

1 To make the syrup, place the sugar and water in a saucepan, bring to a boil and simmer for 10 minutes, until syrupy. Stir in the rose water. Mix together the nuts, confectioners' sugar and cardamom. Preheat the oven to 325°F. Brush a baking pan with butter.

2 Taking one sheet of filo pastry at a time, and keeping the remainder covered with a damp cloth, brush with melted butter and lay on the bottom of the pan. Continue until you have six buttered layers in the pan. Spread half of the nut mixture over, pressing down with a spoon.

3 Take another six sheets of filo pastry, brush with butter and lay over the nut mixture. Sprinkle over the remaining nuts and top with a final layer of six buttered filo sheets. Cut the pastry into small diamond shapes. Pour the remaining butter over the top. Bake for 20 minutes, then increase the heat to 400°F and bake for 15 minutes, until light golden in color and puffed.

4 Remove from the oven and drizzle most of the syrup over the pastry, reserving the remainder for serving.

Almond Cinnamon Balls

These almond balls should be soft inside, with a very strong cinnamon flavor. They harden with keeping, so it is a good idea to freeze some and thaw them when required.

Makes 15

❦

INGREDIENTS

1½ cups ground almonds
⅓ cup granulated sugar
1 tablespoon ground cinnamon
2 egg whites
oil for greasing
confectioners' sugar for dredging

❦

3 Bake for about 15 minutes, so they remain slightly soft inside – too much cooking will make them hard and tough. Slide a metal spatula under the balls to release them from the baking sheet and allow to cool.

4 Sift a few tablespoons of confectioners' sugar onto a plate. When the cinnamon balls are cold, slide them onto the plate. Shake gently to completely cover the cinnamon balls in sugar. Store in an airtight container or in the freezer.

1 Preheat the oven to 350°F. Oil a large baking sheet. Mix together the ground almonds, sugar and cinnamon. Beat the egg whites until they begin to stiffen and fold enough into the almonds to make a fairly firm mixture.

2 Wet your hands with cold water and roll small spoonfuls of the mixture into balls. Place these on the prepared baking sheet.

Biscotti

These lovely Italian biscuits are part-baked, sliced to reveal a feast of mixed nuts and then baked again until crisp and golden. Traditionally they're served dipped in vin santo, *a sweet dessert wine.*

Makes 24

INGREDIENTS

¹/₄ *cup unsalted butter*
¹/₂ *cup sugar*
1¹/₂ *cups self-rising flour*
pinch of salt
2 teaspoons baking powder
1 teaspoon ground coriander
finely grated rind of 1 lemon
¹/₂ *cup medium yellow cornmeal*
1 egg, lightly beaten
2 teaspoons brandy or orange-flavored liqueur
¹/₂ *cup unblanched almonds*
¹/₂ *cup pistachios*

3 Stir in the nuts until evenly combined. Halve the mixture. Shape each half into a flat sausage about 9 inches long and 2¹/₂ inches wide. Bake for about 30 minutes, until risen and firm. Remove from the oven.

1 Preheat the oven to 325°F. Lightly grease a baking sheet. Cream together the butter and sugar in a bowl.

2 Sift the flour, salt, baking powder and coriander into the bowl. Add the lemon rind, cornmeal, egg and brandy or liqueur and mix together to make a soft dough.

4 When cool, cut each sausage diagonally into 12 thin slices. Return to the baking sheet and cook for another 10 minutes, until crisp.

5 Transfer to a wire rack to cool completely. Store in an airtight container for up to one week.

Cook's Tip Use a sharp, serrated knife to slice the cooled biscotti, otherwise they will crumble.

Golden Raisin Cornmeal Cookies

These little yellow cookies come from the Veneto region of Italy.

Makes 48

INGREDIENTS

¹/₂ cup golden raisins
1 cup finely ground yellow cornmeal
1¹/₂ cups all-purpose flour
1¹/₂ teaspoons baking powder
pinch of salt
1 cup butter
1 cup sugar
2 eggs
1 tablespoon marsala or
1 teaspoon vanilla extract

1 Soak the golden raisins in a small bowl of warm water for 15 minutes. Drain. Preheat the oven to 350°F. Grease a baking sheet.

2 Sift the cornmeal, flour, baking powder and salt together into a mixing bowl. Set aside.

3 Cream the butter and sugar until light and fluffy. Beat in the eggs, one at a time. Beat in the marsala or vanilla extract.

4 Add the dry ingredients to the butter mixture, beating until well blended. Stir in the golden raisins.

5 Drop heaping teaspoons of the mixture onto the prepared baking sheet in rows about 2 inches apart. Bake for 7–8 minutes, until the cookies are golden brown at the edges. Transfer to a wire rack to cool.

Amaretti

Almond extract will provide the flavor of bitter almonds, which are not available in the U.S.

Makes 36

INGREDIENTS

1³/₄ cups almonds
flour for dusting
1 cup superfine sugar
2 egg whites
¹/₂ teaspoon almond extract or
1 teaspoon vanilla extract
confectioners' sugar for dusting

1 Preheat the oven to 325°F. Peel the almonds by dropping them into a saucepan of boiling water for 1–2 minutes. Drain. Rub the almonds in a cloth to remove the skins.

2 Place the almonds on a baking sheet and let them dry out in the oven for 10–15 minutes without browning. Remove from the oven and allow to cool. Turn the oven off. Dust the almonds with flour.

3 Grind the almonds with half of the sugar in a food processor. Use an electric beater or wire whisk to beat the egg whites until they form soft peaks.

4 Sprinkle over half the remaining sugar and continue beating until stiff peaks are formed. Gently fold in the remaining sugar, the almond or vanilla extract and the almonds.

5 Spoon the almond mixture into a pastry bag fitted with a smooth nozzle. Pipe out the mixture in rounds the size of a walnut. Sprinkle lightly with the confectioners' sugar, and let stand for 2 hours. Near the end of this time, turn the oven on again and preheat to 350°F.

6 Bake for 15 minutes, until pale gold. Remove from the oven and cool on a wire rack.

Macaroons

Freshly ground almonds, lightly toasted beforehand to intensify the flavor,

give these macaroons their rich taste and texture so, for best results,

avoid using already-ground almonds as a shortcut.

Makes 12

INGREDIENTS

1¹/₂ cup blanched almonds, toasted
³/₄ cup granulated sugar
2 egg whites
¹/₂ teaspoon almond or vanilla extract
confectioners' sugar for dusting

1 Preheat the oven to 350°F. Line a large baking sheet with baking parchment. Reserve 12 almonds for decorating. In a food processor grind the rest of the almonds with the sugar.

2 With the machine running, slowly pour in enough of the egg whites to form a soft dough. Add the almond or vanilla extract and pulse to mix.

3 With moistened hands, shape the mixture into walnut-size balls and arrange on the baking sheet.

4 Press one of the reserved almonds onto each ball, flattening them slightly, and dust lightly with confectioners' sugar. Bake for about 10–12 minutes, until the tops are golden and feel slightly firm. Transfer to a wire rack, cool slightly, then peel the cookies off the paper and allow to cool completely.

Cook's Tip To toast the almonds, spread them on a baking sheet and bake in the preheated oven for 10–15 minutes, until golden. Allow to cool before grinding.

Madeleines

These little tea cakes, baked in a special pan with shell-shaped cups,

were made famous by Marcel Proust, whose great fiction starts off with

the taste of a madeleine.

Makes 12

INGREDIENTS

1¹/₄ cups all-purpose flour
1 teaspoon baking powder
2 eggs
³/₄ cup confectioners' sugar, plus extra for dusting
grated rind of 1 lemon or orange
1 tablespoon lemon or orange juice
6 tablespoons unsalted butter, melted and slightly cooled

1 Preheat the oven to 375°F. Generously butter a 12-cup madeleine pan. Sift together the flour and baking powder.

2 Using an electric mixer, beat the eggs and confectioners' sugar for 5–7 minutes, until thick and creamy and the mixture forms a ribbon when the beaters are lifted. Gently fold in the lemon or orange rind and juice.

3 Beginning with the flour mixture, alternately fold in the flour and melted butter in four batches. Allow the mixture to stand for 10 minutes, then carefully spoon into the pan. Tap gently to release any air bubbles.

4 Bake for 12–15 minutes, rotating the pan halfway through cooking, until a skewer or cake tester inserted in the center comes out clean. Turn onto a wire rack to cool and dust with confectioners' sugar before serving.

Cook's Tip If you don't have a special pan for making madeleines, you can use a muffin pan, preferably with a nonstick coating. The cakes won't have the characteristic ridges and shell shape, but they are quite pretty dusted with a little confectioners' sugar.

Chocolate Macaroons

Makes 24

INGREDIENTS

*2 1-ounce squares semisweet
chocolate
1 cup blanched almonds
1 cup granulated sugar
about 3 egg whites
½ teaspoon vanilla extract
¼ teaspoon almond extract
confectioners' sugar for dusting*

1 Preheat the oven to 325°F. Line two baking sheets with waxed paper and grease the paper.

2 Melt the chocolate in the top of a double boiler, or in a heatproof bowl set over a saucepan of hot water.

3 Grind the almonds finely in a food processor, blender or nut grinder. Transfer to a mixing bowl.

4 Add the sugar, egg whites, vanilla and almond extracts and stir to blend. Stir in the chocolate. The mixture should just hold its shape. If it is too soft, chill for 15 minutes.

5 Use a teaspoon and your hands to shape the dough into walnut-size balls. Place on the prepared baking sheets and flatten slightly.

6 Brush each ball with water and sift over a thin layer of confectioners' sugar. Bake for 10–12 minutes, until just firm. With a metal spatula, transfer to a wire rack to cool.

Variation For Chocolate Pine Nut Macaroons, spread ¼ cup pine nuts in a shallow dish. Press the balls of chocolate macaroon dough into the nuts to cover one side and bake as described, nut-side up.

Coconut Macaroons

Makes 24

INGREDIENTS

*⅓ cup all-purpose flour
pinch of salt
2½ cups dried coconut
⅔ cup sweetened condensed milk
1 teaspoon vanilla extract*

1 Preheat the oven to 350°F. Line two baking sheets with waxed paper and grease the paper.

2 Sift the flour and salt into a large bowl. Stir in the dried coconut.

3 Pour in the sweetened condensed milk. Add the vanilla extract and stir together from the center. Continue stirring until a very thick batter is formed.

4 Drop heaping tablespoonfuls of batter 1 inch apart on the prepared baking sheets. Bake the macaroons for about 20 minutes, until golden brown. Transfer to a wire rack to cool.

Variation For a very rich, sweet and tempting petits four, make the macaroons smaller, and when cooked coat them in melted semisweet chocolate. Place on waxed paper and leave until the chocolate is hard. Serve with small cups of strong, black coffee after a dinner party.

Black-and-White Ginger Florentines

These florentines can be refrigerated in an airtight container for one week.

Makes 30

INGREDIENTS

¹/₂ *cup heavy cream*
¹/₄ *cup unsalted butter*
¹/₂ *cup sugar*
2 *tablespoons honey*
1¹/₃ *cups slivered almonds*
¹/₃ *cup all-purpose flour*
¹/₂ *teaspoon ground ginger*
¹/₃ *cup diced candied orange peel*
¹/₂ *cup diced crystallized ginger*
7 *ounces semisweet chocolate,*
chopped
5 *ounces good-quality white*
chocolate, chopped

3 Drop teaspoons of the mixture onto the prepared baking sheets at least 3 inches apart. Spread each round as thinly as possible with the back of the spoon. (Dip the spoon in water to prevent sticking.)

6 In a small saucepan over a very low heat, melt the remaining chocolate, stirring frequently, until smooth. Cool slightly. In the top of a double boiler over a low heat, melt the white chocolate until smooth, stirring frequently. Remove the top of the double boiler from the bottom and cool for about 5 minutes, stirring occasionally until slightly thickened.

1 Preheat the oven to 350°F. Lightly grease two large baking sheets. In a medium saucepan over medium heat, stir the cream, butter, sugar and honey until the sugar dissolves. Bring the mixture to a boil, stirring constantly.

2 Remove from the heat and stir in the almonds, flour and ground ginger until well blended. Stir in the orange peel, crystallized ginger and ¹/₃ cup chopped semisweet chocolate.

4 Bake in batches for 8–10 minutes, until the edges are golden brown and the cookies are bubbling. Do not underbake or they will be sticky, but be careful not to overbake as they burn easily. If you wish, use a 3-inch cookie cutter to neaten the edges of the florentines while on the baking sheet.

5 Remove the baking sheet to the wire rack to cool for 10 minutes until firm. Using a metal spatula, carefully transfer the florentines to a wire rack to cool completely.

7 Using a small metal spatula, spread half the florentines with the semisweet chocolate on the flat side of each cookie, swirling to create a decorative surface, and place on a wire rack, chocolate side up. Spread the remaining florentines with the melted white chocolate and place on the rack, chocolate side up. Chill for 10–15 minutes to set completely.

Tuiles d'Amandes

These cookies are named after the French roof tiles they so resemble. Making them can be difficult, so bake only four at a time until you get the knack. With a little practice you will find them easy.

Makes 24

INGREDIENTS

generous ¹/₂ cup whole blanched almonds, lightly toasted
¹/₃ cup sugar
3 tablespoons unsalted butter
2 egg whites
¹/₂ teaspoon almond extract
scant ¹/₄ cup all-purpose flour, sifted
¹/₂ cup slivered almonds

Cook's Tip If the tuiles flatten or lose their crispness, reheat them on a baking sheet in a moderate oven until completely flat, then reshape.

1 Preheat the oven to 400°F. Generously butter two heavy baking sheets.

2 Place the almonds and about 2 tablespoons of the sugar in a food processor fitted with the metal blade and process until finely ground.

3 Beat the butter until creamy, then add the remaining sugar and beat until light and fluffy. Gradually beat in the egg whites, then add the almond extract. Sift the flour over the butter mixture, fold in, then fold in the ground almond mixture.

4 Drop tablespoonfuls of the mixture onto the prepared baking sheets about 6 inches apart. With the back of a wet spoon, spread each mound into a paper-thin 3 inch round. (Don't worry if holes appear, they will fill in.) Sprinkle with slivered almonds.

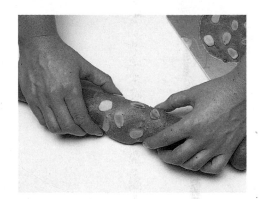

5 Bake the cookies, one sheet at a time, for 5–6 minutes, until the edges are golden and the centers still pale. Working quickly, use a thin spatula to loosen the edges of one cookie. Lift the cookie on the spatula and place over a rolling pin, then press down the sides of the cookie to curve it.

6 Continue shaping the cookies, transferring them to a wire rack as they cool. If they become too crisp to shape, return the baking sheet to the hot oven for 15–30 seconds, then continue as above.

Slivered Almond Cookies

Makes 30

INGREDIENTS

³/₄ cup butter or margarine,
chopped
2 cups self-rising flour
²/₃ cup sugar
¹/₂ teaspoon ground cinnamon
1 egg, separated
2 tablespoons cold water
¹/₂ cup slivered almonds

3 Using a floured fluted round cutter, cut the dough into rounds. Use a metal spatula to lift them onto an ungreased baking sheet. Re-form the dough and cut more rounds to use all the dough. Beat the egg white lightly, brush it over the cookies, and sprinkle over the remaining sugar.

4 Bake for about 10–15 minutes, until golden. To remove, slide a metal spatula under the cookies, which will still seem a bit soft, but they harden as they cool. Let stand on a wire rack until quite cold.

1 Preheat the oven to 350°F. Rub the butter or margarine into the flour. Reserve 1 tablespoon of the sugar and mix the rest with the cinnamon. Stir into the flour and then add the egg yolk and cold water and mix to a firm dough.

2 Roll out the dough on a lightly floured board to ¹/₂ inch thick. Sprinkle over the almonds. Continue rolling until the dough is approximately ¹/₄ inch thick.

Festive and Fancy Cookies

Nut Lace Cookies

Makes 18

INGREDIENTS

½ cup blanched almonds
4 tablespoons butter
3 tablespoons all-purpose flour
½ cup sugar
2 tablespoons heavy cream
½ teaspoon vanilla extract

Variation Add ¼ cup finely chopped candied orange peel to the mixture.

1 Preheat the oven to 375°F. Grease 1–2 baking sheets.

2 With a sharp knife, chop the almonds as finely as possible. Alternatively, use a food processor, blender or nut grinder to chop the nuts very finely.

3 Melt the butter in a small saucepan over low heat. Remove from the heat and stir in the remaining ingredients, including the almonds.

4 Drop teaspoonfuls of the mixture 2½ inches apart on the prepared baking sheets. Bake for about 5 minutes, until golden. Cool on the sheets briefly, until the cookies are just stiff enough to lift off.

5 With a metal spatula, transfer the cookies to a wire rack to cool completely.

Oatmeal Lace Cookies

Makes 36

INGREDIENTS

⅔ cup butter or margarine
1½ cups rolled oats
¾ cup firmly packed dark brown sugar
¾ cup granulated sugar
3 tablespoons all-purpose flour
pinch of salt
1 egg, lightly beaten
1 teaspoon vanilla extract
½ cup pecans or walnuts, finely chopped

1 Preheat the oven to 350°F. Grease two baking sheets.

2 Melt the butter or margarine in a small saucepan over low heat. Set aside.

3 In a mixing bowl, combine the oats, brown sugar, granulated sugar, flour and salt.

4 Add the butter or margarine, the egg and vanilla extract.

5 Mix until blended, then stir in the chopped nuts.

6 Drop rounded teaspoonfuls of the batter about 2 inches apart on the prepared baking sheets. Bake for 5–8 minutes, until lightly browned on the edges and bubbling. Allow to cool for 2 minutes, then transfer to a wire rack to cool completely.

Strawberry Shortcakes

A favorite American summer dessert.

Makes 6

INGREDIENTS

1 pound strawberries, hulled
and halved or quartered,
depending on size
3 tablespoons confectioners' sugar
1 cup heavy cream
mint leaves to decorate
For the shortcakes
2 cups all-purpose flour
⅓ cup superfine sugar
1 tablespoon baking powder
pinch of salt
1 cup heavy cream

Cook's Tip To achieve the best results when whipping cream, chill the bowl and beaters until thoroughly cold. If using an electric mixer, increase the speed gradually, and turn the bowl while beating to incorporate as much air as possible.

1 Preheat the oven to 400°F. Lightly grease a baking sheet.

2 To make the shortcakes, sift the flour into a mixing bowl. Add ¼ cup of the superfine sugar, the baking powder and salt. Stir well.

3 Gradually add the cream, tossing lightly with a fork until the mixture forms clumps.

4 Gather the clumps together, but do not knead the dough. Shape the dough into a 6-inch log. Cut into six slices and place them on the prepared baking sheet.

5 Sprinkle with the remaining superfine sugar. Bake for about 15 minutes, until light golden brown. Allow to cool on a wire rack.

6 Meanwhile, mash a quarter of the strawberries with the confectioners' sugar. Stir in the remaining strawberries. Allow to stand for 1 hour at room temperature.

7 Just before serving, whip the cream until soft peaks form.

8 Slice each shortcake in half. Put the bottom halves on individual plates and top with some of the cream. Divide the strawberries among the six. Replace the tops and decorate with mint. Serve with the remaining cream.

Ladyfingers

Named after the pale, slim fingers of fairy-tale princesses.

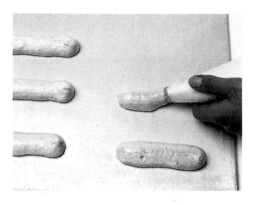

Makes 18

INGREDIENTS

²/₃ cup all-purpose flour
pinch of salt
4 eggs, separated
¹/₂ cup granulated sugar
¹/₂ teaspoon vanilla extract
confectioners' sugar for sprinkling

1 Preheat the oven to 300°F. Grease two baking sheets, then coat lightly with flour, and shake off the excess.

2 Sift the flour and salt together two times.

3 With an electric mixer, beat the egg yolks with half of the sugar until thick enough to leave a ribbon trail when the beaters are lifted.

4 In another bowl, beat the egg whites until stiff. Beat in the remaining sugar until glossy.

5 Sift the flour over the yolks and spoon a large dollop of egg whites over the flour. Carefully fold in with a large metal spoon, adding the vanilla extract. Gently fold in the remaining whites.

6 Spoon the mixture into a pastry bag fitted with a plain nozzle. Pipe 4-inch long lines on the prepared baking sheets about 1 inch apart. Sift over a layer of confectioners' sugar. Turn the sheet upside down to dislodge any excess sugar.

7 Bake for about 20 minutes, until crusty on the outside but soft in the center. Cool slightly on the baking sheets before transferring to a wire rack.

Walnut Cookies

Makes 60

INGREDIENTS

¹/₂ cup butter or margarine
³/₄ cup sugar
1 cup all-purpose flour
2 teaspoons vanilla extract
1 cup walnuts, finely chopped

1 Preheat the oven to 300°F. Grease two baking sheets.

2 With an electric mixer, cream the butter or margarine until soft. Add ¹/₄ cup of the sugar and continue beating until light and fluffy. Stir in the flour, vanilla extract and walnuts. Drop teaspoonfuls of the batter 1–2 inches apart on the prepared baking sheets and flatten slightly. Bake for about 25 minutes.

3 Transfer to a wire rack set over a baking sheet and sprinkle with the remaining sugar.

Variation To make Almond Cookies, use an equal amount of finely chopped unblanched almonds instead of walnuts. Replace half the vanilla with ¹/₂ teaspoon almond extract.

Decorated Chocolate Lebkuchen

Wrapped in paper or cellophane, or beautifully boxed, these decorated cookies make a lovely present. Don't make them too far in advance as the chocolate will gradually discolor.

Makes 40

INGREDIENTS

*1 recipe Lebkuchen mixture
4 ounces semisweet chocolate,
chopped
4 ounces milk chocolate, chopped
4 ounces· white chocolate, chopped
chocolate sprinkles, for sprinkling
cocoa powder or confectioners'
sugar for dusting*

1 Grease two baking sheets. Roll out just over half of the Lebkuchen mixture until ¼ inch thick. Cut out heart shapes, using a 1¾-inch heart-shaped cutter. Transfer to the baking sheets. Gather the trimmings together with the remaining dough and cut into 20 pieces. Roll into balls and place on the baking sheet. Flatten each ball slightly with your fingers.

2 Chill both sheets for 30 minutes. Preheat the oven to 350°F. Bake for 8–10 minutes. Cool on a wire rack.

3 Melt the semisweet chocolate in a heatproof bowl over a small saucepan of hot water. Melt the milk and white chocolate in separate bowls.

4 Make three small paper pastry bags out of waxed paper. Spoon a little of each chocolate into the three paper pastry bags and reserve. Spoon a little semisweet chocolate over one third of the cookies, spreading it slightly to cover them completely. (Tapping the rack gently will help the chocolate to run down the sides.)

5 Snip the merest tip from the bag of white chocolate and drizzle it over some of the coated biscuits, to give a decorative finish.

6 Sprinkle the chocolate sprinkles over the semisweet chocolate-coated cookies that haven't been decorated. Coat the remaining cookies with the milk and white chocolate and decorate some of these with more chocolate from the piping bags, contrasting the colors. Scatter more undecorated cookies with chocolate sprinkles. Allow the cookies to set.

7 Transfer the undecorated cookies to a plate or tray and dust with cocoa powder or confectioners' sugar.

Cook's Tip If the chocolate in the bowls starts to set before you have finished decorating, put the bowls back over the heat for 1–2 minutes. If the chocolate in the pastry bags starts to harden, microwave briefly or put in a clean bowl over a pan of simmering water until soft.

Chocolate Fruit and Nut Cookies

These simple, chunky gingerbread cookies make a delicious gift, especially when presented in a decorative gift box. The combination of walnuts, almonds and cherries is very effective, but you can use any other mixture of candied fruits and nuts.

Makes 20

❦

INGREDIENTS

4 tablespoons granulated sugar
¹/₃ cup water
8 ounces semisweet chocolate, chopped
³/₄ cup walnut halves
¹/₃ cup candied cherries, chopped into small wedges
1 cup whole blanched almonds
For the Lebkuchen
¹/₂ cup unsalted butter
²/₃ cup firmly packed light brown sugar
1 egg, beaten
¹/₃ cup molasses
3¹/₂ cups self-rising flour
1 teaspoon ground ginger
¹/₂ teaspoon ground cloves
¹/₄ teaspoon cayenne pepper

❦

Cook's Tip Carefully stack the cookies in a pretty box or tin, lined with tissue paper, or tie in cellophane bundles.

1 To make the Lebkuchen, cream together the butter and sugar until pale and fluffy. Beat in the egg and molasses. Sift the flour, ginger, cloves and cayenne pepper into the bowl. Using a wooden spoon, gradually mix the ingredients together to make a stiff paste. Turn onto a lightly floured work surface and knead lightly until smooth. Wrap and chill for 30 minutes.

2 Preheat the oven to 350°F. Grease two baking sheets. Shape the dough into a roll, 8 inches long. Chill for 30 minutes. Cut into 20 slices and space them on the baking sheets. Bake for 10 minutes. Leave on the baking sheets for 5 minutes and then transfer to a wire rack and set aside to cool.

3 Put the sugar and water in a small, heavy-bottomed saucepan. Heat gently until the sugar dissolves. Bring to a boil and boil for 1 minute, until slightly syrupy. Leave for 3 minutes, to cool slightly, and then stir in the chocolate until it has melted and made a smooth sauce.

4 Place the wire rack of cookies over a large tray or board. Spoon a little of the chocolate mixture over the cookies, spreading it to the edges with the back of the spoon.

5 Gently press a walnut half into the center of each cookie. Arrange pieces of candied cherry and almonds alternately around the nuts. Allow to set in a cool place.

Chocolate Almond Torrone

Serve this Italian speciality in thin slices.

Makes 20

❦

INGREDIENTS

*4 ounces semisweet chocolate,
chopped
4 tablespoons unsalted butter
1 egg white
$^{1}/_{2}$ cup superfine sugar
$^{1}/_{2}$ cup ground almonds
$^{3}/_{4}$ cup chopped almonds, toasted
5 tablespoons chopped candied peel
For the coating
6 ounces white chocolate, chopped
2 tablespoons unsalted butter
1 cup slivered almonds, toasted*

❦

1 Melt the chocolate with the butter in a heatproof bowl over a saucepan of hot water, stirring until the mixture is smooth.

2 In a clean, grease-free bowl, beat the egg white with the sugar until stiff. Gradually beat in the melted chocolate, then stir in the ground almonds, chopped toasted almonds and chopped peel.

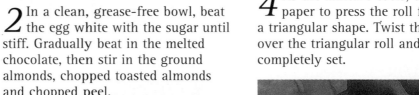

3 Tip the mixture onto a large sheet of baking parchment and shape into a thick roll.

4 As the mixture cools, use the paper to press the roll firmly into a triangular shape. Twist the paper over the triangular roll and chill until completely set.

5 To make the coating, melt the white chocolate with the butter in a heatproof bowl over a saucepan of hot water. Unwrap the chocolate roll and spread the white chocolate quickly over the surface. Press the slivered almonds in a thin, even coat over the chocolate, working quickly before the chocolate sets.

6 Chill again until firm, then cut the torrone into fairly thin slices to serve.

Cook's Tip The mixture can be shaped into a simple round roll instead of the triangular shape if you prefer.

116

Chocolate Hazelnut Galettes

*There's stacks of sophistication in these triple-tiered chocolate rounds
sandwiched with a light fromage blanc filling.*

Makes 4

INGREDIENTS

6 ounces semisweet chocolate,
chopped
3 tablespoons light cream
2 tablespoons slivered hazelnuts
4 ounces white chocolate, chopped
³⁄₄ cup fromage blanc
1 tablespoon dry sherry
4 tablespoons finely chopped
hazelnuts, toasted
physalis (Cape gooseberries),
dipped in white chocolate,
to decorate

1 Melt the semisweet chocolate in a heatproof bowl over a saucepan of hot water, then remove from the heat and stir in the cream.

2 Draw 12 3-inch circles on sheets of baking parchment. Turn the paper over and spread the semisweet chocolate over each marked circle, covering in a thin, even layer. Scatter slivered hazelnuts over four of the circles, then put aside until set.

3 Melt the white chocolate in a heatproof bowl over a saucepan of hot water, then stir in the fromage blanc and dry sherry. Fold in the chopped, toasted hazelnuts. Allow to cool until the mixture holds its shape.

Cook's Tip If gooseberries aren't available, raspberries or blackberries make delicious substitutes.

4 Remove the semisweet chocolate rounds carefully from the paper and sandwich them together in stacks of 3, spooning the white chocolate hazelnut cream between each layer and using the hazelnut-covered rounds on top. Chill before serving.

5 To serve, place the galettes on individual plates and decorate with chocolate-dipped physalis.

Savory
Treats

The earliest cookies were savory, made with just flour, water and perhaps some salt, but as the practice of cookie-making became established the savory version lost ground to sweet cookies. Now, there is a trend toward more savory tastes with more wine being drunk, and quaffed more casually rather than consumed only as an accompaniment to special meals, so savory cookies, often called biscuits, are making a comeback. This time, though, the recipes are far more varied and appetizing. Variety is introduced by using different flours, and including ingredients such as oats, cornmeal and nuts for texture. Savory cookie doughs are flavored with cheese, herbs and spices, or topped with sesame or other seeds for extra crunch and savor.

Try sandwiching savory cookies together in pairs with soft cheese, simply seasoned or flavored with a complementary ingredient, such as chives with cheese biscuits. Triple-deckers can be created in the same way. Avoid filling cookies too far in advance, though, in case they soften.

Any type of savory cookie is versatile — it can be served with drinks, soups and cheese, or taken in packed lunches and picnics.

Festive Nibbles

Shape these spicy cheese snacks in any way you wish –

stars, crescent moons, triangles, squares, hearts,

fingers or rounds. Serve them with drinks from

ice-cold cocktails to hot and spicy mulled wine and spirits.

Makes 60

INGREDIENTS

1 cup all-purpose flour, plus
extra for dusting
1 teaspoon dry mustard
pinch of salt
1/2 cup butter
3/4 cup Cheddar cheese, grated
pinch of cayenne pepper
2 tablespoons water
1 egg, beaten
poppy seeds, sunflower seeds or
sesame seeds, to decorate

1 Preheat the oven to 400°F. Grease two baking sheets. Sift the flour, dry mustard and salt into a bowl and rub in the butter until the mixture resembles fine bread crumbs.

2 Stir in the cheese and cayenne pepper and sprinkle on the water. Add half the beaten egg, mix to a firm dough and knead lightly until smooth.

3 Roll out the dough on a lightly floured surface and cut out a variety of shapes. Re-roll the trimmings and cut more shapes.

4 Place on the prepared baking sheets and brush with the remaining egg. Sprinkle on the seeds. Bake for 8–10 minutes, until golden.

Cheese Straws

Makes 50 straws and 8 rings

INGREDIENTS

1 cup all-purpose flour, plus
extra for dusting
1 teaspoon mustard powder
pinch of salt
1/2 cup butter
3/4 cup Cheddar cheese, grated
pinch of cayenne pepper
2 tablespoons water
1 egg, beaten
poppy seeds, sunflower seeds or
sesame seeds, to decorate

1 Make the cheese pastry in the same way as Festive Nibbles. Cut the cheese pastry into fingers about 4 inches long and 1/4 inch wide.

2 Roll out the trimmings, cut rounds using two pastry cutters of different sizes. a 2 1/2 inch one to cut out the circle and a 2 inch diameter one to stamp out the center. Cook as above.

3 To serve, push six or eight straws through each ring.

Bacon Twists

Making bread is always fun, so try this savory version and add that extra twist to breakfast.
Serve with soft cheese with herbs.

Makes 12

INGREDIENTS

4 cups all-purpose flour
1 envelope easy-blend active
dry yeast
pinch of salt
1²/₃ cups hand-hot water
12 lean bacon strips
1 egg, beaten

Cook's Tip The same basic dough mix can be used to make rolls or a loaf of bread. Tap the base of the loaf — if it sounds hollow, it's cooked.

2 Turn the dough onto a lightly floured surface and knead for 5 minutes, until the dough is smooth and elastic.

4 Place each bacon strip on a chopping board and run the back of the knife down its length, to stretch it slightly. Wind a strip of bacon around each dough "sausage."

1 Mix the flour, yeast and salt in a bowl and stir them together. Add a little of the water and mix with a knife. Add the remaining water and use your hands to pull the mixture together, to make a sticky dough.

3 Divide the dough into 12 even-size pieces and roll each one into a sausage shape. Lightly oil a baking sheet.

5 Brush the "sausages" with beaten egg and arrange them on the prepared baking sheet. Set aside in a warm place for 30 minutes, until doubled in size. Preheat the oven to 400°F. Bake the "sausages" for 20–25 minutes, until cooked and browned.

Variations Make some meat-free versions of these twists for vegetarians by twisting the dough by hand and sprinkling with poppy or sesame seeds before baking.

Wisconsin Cheddar and Chive Biscuits

These soft biscuits are delicious warm, split and spread with butter;

serve with soup or a main dish.

Makes 20

INGREDIENTS

1³/₄ cups all-purpose flour
2 teaspoons baking powder
¹/₂ teaspoon baking soda
pinch of salt
¹/₄ teaspoon black pepper
5 tablespoons unsalted butter, chopped
¹/₂ cup grated aged Cheddar cheese
2 tablespoons chopped fresh chives
³/₄ cup buttermilk

Variation For Cheddar and Bacon Biscuits, substitute 3 tablespoons crumbled cooked bacon for the chives.

1 Preheat the oven to 400°F. Grease a baking sheet.

2 Sift the flour, baking powder, baking soda, salt and pepper into a large bowl. Rub the butter into the dry ingredients until the mixture resembles coarse bread crumbs. Add the cheese and chives and stir to mix.

3 Make a well in the center of the mixture. Add the buttermilk and stir vigorously until the batter comes away from the sides of the bowl.

4 Drop in 2 tablespoon mounds spaced 2–3 inches apart on the prepared baking sheet. Bake for 12–15 minutes, until golden brown.

Corn Oysters

Serve hot by themselves or as an accompaniment to meat or chicken dishes.

Makes about 8

INGREDIENTS

1 cup grated fresh corn kernels
1 egg, separated
2 tablespoons all-purpose flour
pinch of salt
¹/₄ teaspoon black pepper
2–4 tablespoons butter or margarine
2–4 tablespoons vegetable oil

1 Combine the corn, egg yolk and flour in a bowl. Mix well. Add the salt and pepper.

2 In a separate bowl, beat the egg white until it forms stiff peaks. Fold it carefully into the corn mixture.

3 Heat 2 tablespoons butter or margarine with 2 tablespoons oil in a frying pan. When the fats are very hot and almost smoking, drop tablespoonfuls of the corn mixture into the pan. Fry until crisp and brown on the undersides.

4 Turn the "oysters" over and cook for 1–2 minutes on the other side. Drain on paper towels and keep hot. Continue frying the "oysters," adding more fat as necessary.

Cook's Tip Thawed frozen or canned corn kernels can also be used. Drain them well and chop.

Salted Peanut Cookies

The combinaton of salt and sweet flavors is delicfous.

Makes 70

❧

INGREDIENTS

3 cups all-purpose flour
¹/₂ teaspoon baking soda
¹/₂ cup butter
¹/₂ cup margarine
1¹/₂ cups light brown sugar
2 eggs
2 teaspoons vanilla extract
2 cups salted peanuts

❧

1 Preheat the oven to 375°F. Lightly grease two baking sheets. Grease the bottom of a glass and dip it in sugar.

2 Sift together the flour and baking soda. Set aside.

3 With an electric mixer, cream the butter, margarine and sugar until light and fluffy. Beat in the eggs and vanilla extract. Fold in the flour mixture.

Variation To make Cashew Cookies, substitute an equal amount of salted cashews for the peanuts, and add as above. The flavor is subtle and interesting.

4 Stir the peanuts into the butter mixture until evenly combined.

5 Drop teaspoonfuls 2 inches apart on the prepared sheets. Flatten with the prepared glass.

6 Bake for about 10 minutes, until lightly colored. With a metal spatula, transfer to a wire rack to cool completely.

Cheddar Pennies

Serve these tasty snacks with pre-dinner drinks.

Makes 20

❧

INGREDIENTS

4 tablespoons butter
1 cup Cheddar cheese, grated
¹/₃ cup all-purpose flour
pinch of salt
pinch of cayenne pepper

❧

1 With an electric mixer, cream the butter until soft.

2 Stir in the cheese, flour, salt and cayenne. Gather to form a dough.

3 Transfer to a lightly floured surface. Shape into a cylinder about 1¹/₄ inches in diameter. Wrap in waxed paper and chill for 1–2 hours.

4 Preheat the oven to 350°F. Grease 1–2 baking sheets.

5 Cut the dough into ¹/₄ inch thick slices and place on the prepared baking sheets. Bake for about 15 minutes, until golden. Transfer to a wire rack to cool.

Blue Cheese and Chive Crisps

Makes 48

INGREDIENTS

2 cups blue cheese, crumbled
¹/₂ cup unsalted butter
1 egg
1 egg yolk
2 teaspoons chopped fresh chives
black pepper
2 cups all-purpose flour, sifted

1 The day before serving, beat together the cheese and butter until well blended. Add the egg, egg yolk, chives and a little pepper and beat until just blended.

2 Add the flour in three batches, folding in well between each addition.

Cook's Tip The cheese crisps will keep up to 10 days in an airtight container.

3 Divide the dough in half and shape each half into a log about 2 inches in diameter. Wrap in waxed paper and chill overnight. Preheat the oven to 375°F. Lightly grease two baking sheets.

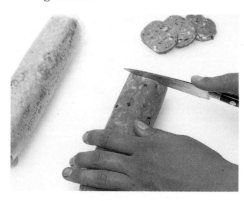

4 Cut the dough logs across into slices about ¹/₈ inch thick. Place on the prepared baking sheets. Bake for about 10 minutes, until just golden around the edges. Transfer to a wire rack to cool.

Cheese Muffins

Makes 9

❦

INGREDIENTS

4 tablespoons butter
1¹/₂ cups all-purpose flour
2 teaspoons baking powder
2 tablespoons sugar
pinch of salt
1 teaspoon paprika
2 eggs
¹/₂ cup milk
1 teaspoon dried thyme
2 ounces aged Cheddar cheese, cut
into ¹/₂-inch dice

❦

1 Preheat the oven to 375°F. Grease nine muffin tins, or use paper liners. Melt the butter in a small saucepan.

2 In a mixing bowl, sift together the flour, baking powder, sugar, salt and paprika.

3 In another bowl, combine the eggs, milk, melted butter and thyme and whisk to blend.

4 Add the milk mixture to the dry ingredients and stir until just moistened; do not mix until smooth.

5 Place a heaping spoonful of batter into the prepared pans. Drop a few pieces of cheese over each, then top with another spoonful of batter.

6 Bake for about 25 minutes, until puffed and golden. Allow to stand for 5 minutes before unmolding onto a wire rack. These muffins are best served warm or at room temperature.

Bacon Cornmeal Muffins

Serve these muffins fresh from the oven for a special breakfast.

Makes 14

❦

INGREDIENTS

8 bacon strips
4 tablespoons butter
4 tablespoons margarine
1 cup all-purpose flour
1 tablespoon baking powder
1 teaspoon sugar
pinch of salt
1¹/₂ cups cornmeal
1 cup milk
2 eggs

❦

1 Preheat the oven to 400°F. Grease 14 muffin pans, or use paper liners.

2 Fry the bacon until crisp. Drain on paper towels, then chop into small pieces. Set aside. Melt the butter and margarine in a saucepan over low heat and set aside.

3 Sift the flour, baking powder, sugar and salt into a large mixing bowl. Stir in the cornmeal, then make a well in the center. In another saucepan, heat the milk to lukewarm. In a small bowl, lightly beat the eggs, then add to the milk. Stir in the melted fats.

4 Pour the milk mixture into the center of the well and stir until smooth and well blended.

5 Fold in the bacon. Spoon the batter into the prepared pans, filling them halfway. Bake for about 20 minutes, until risen and lightly colored.

Savory Parmesan Puffs

Makes 6

❦

INGREDIENTS

¹/₂ cup freshly grated Parmesan
cheese
1 cup all-purpose flour
pinch of salt
1 tablespoon butter or margarine
2 eggs
1 cup milk

❦

1 Preheat the oven to 450°F. Grease six individual baking tins. Sprinkle each pan with 1 tablespoon of the grated Parmesan. Alternatively, you can use ramekins, in which case, heat them on a baking sheet in the oven, then grease and sprinkle with Parmesan just before filling. Sift the flour and salt into a small bowl. Set aside. Melt the butter or margarine in a small saucepan.

2 In a mixing bowl, beat together the eggs, milk and melted butter or margarine. Add the flour mixture and stir until smoothly blended.

3 Divide the batter evenly among the containers, filling each one about half full. Bake for 15 minutes, then sprinkle the tops of the puffs with the remaining grated Parmesan cheese. Reduce the heat to 350°F and continue baking for 20–25 minutes, until the puffs are firm and golden brown.

4 Remove the puffs from the oven. To unmold, run a thin knife around the inside of each container to loosen them. Gently ease out, then transfer to a wire rack to cool.

Herb Popovers

Makes 12

INGREDIENTS

2 tablespoons butter
3 eggs
1 cup milk
³/₄ cup all-purpose flour
pinch of salt
1 small sprig each mixed fresh herbs, such as chives, tarragon, dill and parsley

1 Preheat the oven to 425°F. Grease 12 small ramekins or popover pans. Melt the butter in a small saucepan over low heat.

2 With an electric mixer, beat the eggs until blended. Beat in the milk and melted butter.

3 Sift together the flour and salt, then beat into the egg mixture to combine thoroughly.

4 Strip the herb leaves from the stems and chop finely. Stir 2 tablespoons into the batter.

5 Pour the batter into the dishes or pans so they are half full.

6 Bake for 25–30 minutes, until golden. Do not open the oven door during baking time or the popovers may fall. For drier popovers, pierce each one with a knife after 30 minutes baking time and bake for 5 minutes more. Serve hot.

Cheese Popovers

Makes 12

INGREDIENTS

1¹/₂ tablespoons butter
3 eggs
1 cup milk
³/₄ cup all-purpose flour
pinch of salt
¹/₄ teaspoon paprika
6 tablespoons freshly grated Parmesan cheese

1 Preheat the oven to 425°F. Grease 12 small ramekins or popover pans. Melt the butter in a small saucepan over low heat.

2 With an electric mixer, beat the eggs until blended. Beat in the milk and melted butter.

3 Sift together the flour, salt, and paprika, then beat into the egg mixture. Add the cheese and stir.

4 Fill the prepared dishes or pans so they are half full. Bake for 25–30 minutes, until golden. Do not open the oven door during baking or the popovers will fall. For drier popovers, pierce each one with a knife after 30 minutes baking time and bake for 5 minutes more. Serve hot.

Tiny Cheese Puffs

These bite-sized portions of choux pastry are the ideal accompaniment
to a glass of wine before dinner.

Makes 45

INGREDIENTS

1 cup all-purpose flour
pinch of salt
1 teaspoon dry mustard
pinch of cayenne pepper
1 cup water
¹/₂ cup butter, chopped
4 eggs
3 ounces Gruyère or Swiss cheese,
finely diced
1 tablespoon finely chopped
chives

Cook's Tip The puffs can be prepared ahead and are suitable for freezing. Reheat in a hot oven for 5 minutes, until crisp, before serving.

1 Preheat the oven to 400°F. Lightly grease two large baking sheets. Sift together the flour, salt, dry mustard and cayenne pepper.

2 In a medium-sized saucepan, bring the water and butter to a boil over medium-high heat. Remove from the heat and add the flour mixture all at once, beating with a wooden spoon until the dough forms a ball. Return to the heat and beat constantly for 1–2 minutes to dry out. Remove from the heat and cool for 3–5 minutes.

3 Beat three of the eggs into the dough, one at a time, beating well after each addition. Beat the fourth egg in a small bowl and add a teaspoon at a time, beating until the dough is smooth and shiny and falls slowly when dropped from a spoon. (You may not need all of the fourth egg; reserve any remaining egg for glazing.) Stir in the diced cheese and chives.

4 Using two teaspoons, drop small mounds of dough 2 inches apart onto the prepared baking sheets. Beat the reserved egg with 1 tablespoon water and brush the tops with the glaze.

5 Bake for 8 minutes, then reduce the oven temperature to 350°F and bake for 7–8 minutes more, until puffed and golden. Transfer to a wire rack to cool. Serve warm.

Variation For Ham and Cheese Puffs, add ¹/₄ cup finely diced ham with the cheese. For Cheese Herb Puffs, stir in 2 tablespoons chopped fresh herbs or scallions with the cheese.

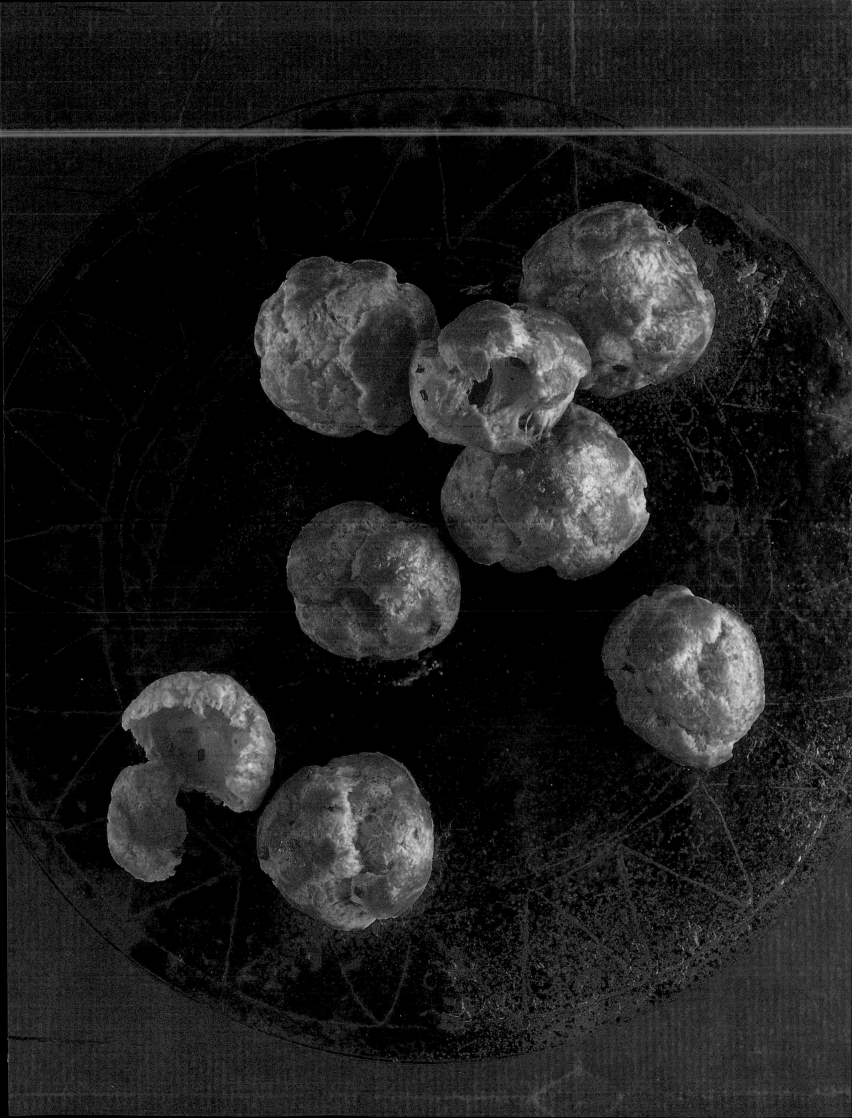

Cheese Biscuits

These delicious biscuits make a good tea-time treat. They are best served fresh and still slightly warm.

Makes 12

INGREDIENTS

2 cups all-purpose flour
2 1/2 teaspoons baking powder
1/2 teaspoon dry mustard
1/2 teaspoon salt
4 tablespoons cold butter, chopped
3/4 cup Cheddar cheese, grated
2/3 cup milk
1 egg, beaten

1 Preheat the oven to 450°F. Sift the flour, baking powder, dry mustard and salt into a mixing bowl. Add the butter and rub into the flour mixture until the mixture resembles bread crumbs.

2 Stir in 1/2 cup of the cheese into the butter and flour mixture.

3 Make a well in the center and gently stir in the milk and egg until smooth. Turn the dough onto a lightly floured surface.

4 Roll out the dough and cut into triangles or squares. Brush lightly with milk and sprinkle with the remaining cheese. Allow to rest for 15 minutes, then bake for 15 minutes, until well risen.

Oatcakes

These are very simple to make and are an excellent addition to a cheese board.

Makes 24

INGREDIENTS

2 cups rolled oats, plus extra for sprinkling
1/4 cup all-purpose flour
1/4 teaspoon baking soda
1 teaspoon salt
2 tablespoons vegetable shortening
2 tablespoons butter

1 Preheat the oven to 425°F. Place the oats, flour, baking soda and salt in a large bowl. Melt the two fats together in a small saucepan over low heat.

2 Add the melted fat and enough boiling water to make a dough. Turn onto a surface sprinkled with a little oatmeal. Roll out thinly and cut into 24 circles. Bake on ungreased baking sheets for 15 minutes.

Ham and Sun-Dried Tomato Biscuits

These make an ideal accompaniment for soup. Choose a strongly flavored ham and chop it fairly finely, so that a little goes a long way.

Makes 12

❦

INGREDIENTS

2 cups self-rising flour
1 teaspoon dry mustard
1 teaspoon paprika, plus extra
for sprinkling
pinch of salt
2 tablespoons margarine, chopped
1 tablespoon snipped fresh basil
¹/₃ cup drained sun-dried tomatoes
in oil, chopped
2 ounces Black Forest or Virginia
ham, chopped
¹/₄–¹/₂ cup skim milk, plus extra
for brushing

❦

1 Preheat the oven to 400°F. Flour a large baking sheet. Sift the flour, mustard, paprika and salt into a bowl. Using your fingers, rub in the margarine until the mixture resembles bread crumbs.

2 Stir the basil, sun-dried tomatoes and ham into the bowl. Pour in enough milk to make a soft dough.

3 Turn the dough onto a lightly floured surface, knead lightly and roll out to an 8 x 6-inch rectangle. Cut into 2-inch squares and arrange on the baking sheet.

4 Brush the tops with milk, sprinkle with paprika and bake for 12–15 minutes. Transfer to a rack to cool.

142

Feta Cheese and Chive Biscuits

Feta cheese makes an excellent substitute for butter in these tangy savory biscuits.

Makes 9

❦

INGREDIENTS

1 cup self-rising white flour
1 cup self-rising whole wheat flour
pinch of salt
3 ounces feta cheese
1 tablespoon chopped fresh chives
²/₃ cup skim milk, plus extra for glazing
¹/₄ teaspoon cayenne pepper

❦

1 Preheat the oven to 400°F. Sift the flours and salt into a mixing bowl, adding any bran left over from the flour in the sieve.

2 Crumble the feta cheese and rub into the dry ingredients. Stir in the chives, then add the milk and mix to a soft dough.

3 Turn onto a floured surface and lightly knead until smooth. Roll out to ³/₄-inch thick and stamp out nine biscuits with a floured 2¹/₂-inch cookie cutter.

4 Transfer to a nonstick baking sheet. Brush with skim milk, then sprinkle over the cayenne pepper. Bake for 15 minutes, until golden brown. Serve warm or cold.

143

Whole Wheat Herb Triangles

Stuffed with cooked chicken and salad, these make a good lunchtime snack, and are also an

ideal accompaniment to a bowl of steaming soup.

Makes 8

🌿

INGREDIENTS

2 cups whole wheat flour
1 cup all-purpose flour
pinch of salt
¹/₂ teaspoon baking soda
1 teaspoon cream of tartar
¹/₂ teaspoon cayenne pepper
¹/₄ cup margarine, chopped
4 tablespoons chopped mixed
fresh herbs
1 cup skim milk
1 tablespoon sesame seeds

🌿

1 Preheat the oven to 425°F. Lightly flour a baking sheet. Put the whole wheat flour and all-purpose flour in a mixing bowl. Sift in the salt, baking soda, cream of tartar and cayenne pepper, then rub in the margarine.

2 Add the herbs and milk and mix quickly to a soft dough. Turn onto a lightly floured surface. Knead only very briefly or the dough will become tough.

3 Roll the dough out to a 9-inch round and place on the prepared baking sheet. Brush lightly with water and sprinkle the top evenly with the sesame seeds.

4 Carefully cut the dough round into eight wedges, separate them slightly and bake for 15–20 minutes. Transfer to a wire rack to cool. Serve warm or cold.

Variation To make Sun-Dried Tomato Triangles, replace the fresh mixed herbs with 2 tablespoons drained chopped sun-dried tomatoes in oil, and add 1 tablespoon each mild paprika, chopped fresh parsley and chopped fresh marjoram.

Dill and Potato Cakes

Makes 10

❧

INGREDIENTS

2 cups self-rising flour
3 tablespoons butter
pinch of salt
1 tablespoon finely chopped fresh
dill
scant 1 cup mashed potato,
freshly made
2–3 tablespoons milk

❧

1 Preheat the oven to 450°F. Sift the flour into a bowl, and add the butter, salt and dill. Mix in the potato and enough milk to make a soft dough.

2 Roll out the dough until fairly thin. Cut into neat rounds with a floured 3-inch cutter. Place the cakes on a greased baking sheet, and bake for 20–25 minutes.

Brownies
and Bars

A brownie should be a moist, chewy bar, crisp on the outside but slightly underdone inside. There are many recipes for brownies, varying in richness.

Bars are the quickest and easiest cookies to shape evenly. The cookie mixture is simply poured or pressed into the pan, baked, then cut to the required size with a large, sharp knife while still warm from the oven.

Some bar cookies are just a single layer, while others are double- or even triple-layered. The layers are sometimes added before baking, sometimes part way through the cooking, depending on the recipe.

Try to use the size pan stated in a recipe. If you use one that is smaller, the layer of mixture will be deeper so the outside of the bars will become overcooked and too brown and crisp or hard before the inside is ready, whereas if too large a pan is used the mixture will be spread too thinly, and not only will it cook too quickly and dry out, but the contrast of moist center to crisp crust will be lessened. If you only have a larger pan, the size can be reduced by making a wide strip formed from a triple thickness of foil to fit across the pan at the right place. Fold up along a long edge to make a lap that the weight of the mixture will hold down, keeping the foil divider in place.

Bar cookies can be stored for a day or so in their baking pan. Cover the pan as tightly as you can with foil, or slide it into a plastic bag, gently press out as much air as possible and seal tightly.

White Chocolate Brownies

Makes 16

❧

INGREDIENTS

1¼ cups all-purpose flour
½ teaspoon baking powder
pinch of salt
6 ounces good-quality white
chocolate, chopped
½ cup sugar
½ cup unsalted butter, chopped
2 eggs, lightly beaten
1 teaspoon vanilla extract
6 ounces semisweet chocolate,
chopped; or chocolate chips
For the topping
7 ounces milk chocolate, chopped
2 cups unsalted macadamia nuts,
chopped

❧

1 Preheat the oven to 350°F. Grease a 9-inch springform pan. Sift together the flour, baking powder and salt. Set aside.

2 In a medium saucepan over medium heat, melt the white chocolate, sugar and butter, stirring until smooth.

3 Cool slightly, then beat in the eggs and vanilla extract. Stir in the flour until well blended. Stir in the chopped chocolate or chocolate chips. Spread evenly in the prepared pan, smoothing the top.

4 Bake for 20–25 minutes, until a skewer inserted 2 inches from the side of the pan comes out clean. Remove from the oven. Sprinkle chopped milk chocolate evenly over the surface (avoid touching the side of the pan) and return to the oven for 1 minute.

5 Remove from the oven and, using the back of a spoon, spread the softened chocolate evenly over the top. Sprinkle with the macadamia nuts and gently press into the chocolate. Cool on a wire rack for 30 minutes, then chill until set. Run a sharp knife around the side of the pan to loosen; unclip the pan side and carefully remove. Cut into thin wedges.

Marbled Brownies

Makes 24

INGREDIENTS

*8 ounces semisweet chocolate,
chopped
¹/₃ cup butter, chopped
4 eggs
1¹/₂ cups sugar
1 cup all-purpose flour
pinch of salt
1 teaspoon baking powder
2 teaspoons vanilla extract
1 cup walnuts, chopped
For the plain batter
4 tablespoons butter
²/₃ cup cream cheese
¹/₂ cup sugar
2 eggs
2 tablespoons all-purpose flour
1 teaspoon vanilla extract*

1 Preheat the oven to 350°F.
Line a 13 x 9-inch pan
with waxed paper and grease
the paper.

2 Melt the chocolate and butter in a
saucepan over very low heat.

3 Meanwhile, beat the eggs until
light and fluffy. Gradually add
the sugar and continue beating until
blended. Sift over the flour, salt and
baking powder and fold in.

4 Stir in the cooled chocolate
mixture and the vanilla extract
and walnuts. Set aside 2 cups of the
chocolate batter.

5 To make the plain batter, cream
the butter and cream cheese with
an electric mixer.

6 Add the sugar and continue
beating until blended. Beat in the
eggs, flour and vanilla extract.

7 Spread the unmeasured chocolate
batter into the pan. Pour over the
cream cheese mixture. Drop spoonfuls
of the reserved chocolate batter on top.

8 With a metal spatula, swirl the
mixtures to marble. Do not blend
completely. Bake for 35–40 minutes,
until just set. Unmold when cool and
cut into squares for serving.

Fudge-Glazed Chocolate Slices

Makes 8–10

◖

INGREDIENTS

11 ounces semisweet chocolate,
chopped
¹/₂ cup unsalted butter, chopped
generous ¹/₂ cup firmly packed
light brown sugar
¹/₄ cup granulated sugar
2 eggs
1 tablespoon vanilla extract
¹/₂ cup all-purpose flour
1 cup pecans or walnuts, toasted
and chopped
5 ounces good-quality white
chocolate, chopped
For the Fudge Glaze
6 ounces semisweet chocolate,
chopped
4 tablespoons unsalted butter,
chopped
2 tablespoons light corn syrup
2 teaspoons vanilla extract
1 teaspoon instant coffee powder
pecan halves, to decorate
(optional)

◖

1 Preheat the oven to 350°F. Invert an 8-inch square baking pan and mold a piece of foil over the bottom. Turn the pan over and line with molded foil. Lightly grease the foil.

2 In a medium saucepan over low heat, melt the semisweet chocolate and butter, stirring until smooth.

3 Stir in the sugars and continue stirring for 2 minutes, until the sugar has dissolved. Beat in the eggs and vanilla extract. Stir in the flour, nuts and white chocolate. Pour the batter into the prepared pan.

4 Bake for 20–25 minutes, until a skewer inserted 2 inches from the center comes out clean. Remove the pan to a wire rack to cool for 30 minutes. Using the foil, lift from the pan and cool on the wire rack for 2 hours.

5 To make the glaze, melt the chocolate, butter, syrup, vanilla extract and coffee powder in a medium saucepan over medium heat, stirring frequently, until smooth. Remove from the heat. Chill for 1 hour, until thickened and spreadable.

6 Invert the cake onto the wire rack, and remove the foil from the bottom. Turn top side up. Using a metal spatula, spread a thick layer of fudge glaze over the top of the cake just to the edges. Chill for 1 hour, until set. Cut into squares or fingers. If you wish, top each with a pecan half.

Chocolate Brownies

Wonderful old-fashioned brownies are usually high in fat. This no-butter version still tastes rich and mellow but is best eaten on the day it is made.

Makes 20

INGREDIENTS

½ cup sunflower oil
5 ounces semisweet chocolate, chopped
2 eggs
1 cup self-rising flour
½ cup sugar
1 teaspoon vanilla extract
¾ cup halved pecans

1 Preheat the oven to 400°F. Use a little of the oil to grease a 9-inch square shallow cake pan and line with lightly oiled waxed paper.

Cook's Tip Ingredients can be melted easily in the microwave. To soften chocolate, butter, sugar or syrup, microwave on full power for a few minutes, until soft.

2 Melt the chocolate with the remaining oil in a heatproof bowl over a saucepan of water, stirring until smooth.

3 Beat the eggs lightly and add them to the chocolate, stirring vigorously. Beat in the flour, sugar and vanilla extract and pour the mixture into the prepared pan. Arrange the pecans over the top.

4 Bake for 10–15 minutes. If you like chewy brownies, take them out of the oven now. If you want a more cake-like finish, leave for another 5 minutes. Cut into squares and allow to cool before removing from the pan.

Nut and Chocolate Chip Brownies

These brownies are moist, dark and deeply satisfying.

Makes 16

INGREDIENTS

5 ounces semisweet chocolate, chopped
½ cup sunflower oil
1¼ cups firmly packed light brown sugar
2 eggs
1 teaspoon vanilla extract
⅔ cup self-rising flour
4 tablespoons cocoa powder
¼ cup chopped walnuts or pecans
4 tablespoons milk chocolate chips

Cook's Tip These brownies will freeze for 3 months in an airtight container.

1 Preheat the oven to 350°F. Lightly grease a shallow 7½-inch square cake pan. Melt the semisweet chocolate in a heatproof bowl over a saucepan of hot water.

2 With an electric mixer, beat the oil, sugar, eggs and vanilla extract together in a large bowl.

3 Stir in the melted chocolate, then beat well until evenly mixed.

4 Sift the flour and cocoa powder into the bowl and fold in thoroughly. Stir in the chopped nuts and chocolate chips, pour into the prepared pan and spread evenly to the edges. Bake for 30–35 minutes, until the top is firm and crusty. Cool in the pan before cutting into squares.

Banana Gingerbread

This gingerbread keeps well and actually improves with age. Store it in a covered container for up to 2 months.

Makes 26

INGREDIENTS

1¾ cups all-purpose flour
2 teaspoons baking soda
2 teaspoons ground ginger
1¾ cups rolled oats
4 tablespoons dark brown sugar
⅓ cup margarine, chopped
⅔ cup light corn syrup
1 egg, beaten
3 ripe bananas, mashed
¾ cup confectioners' sugar
crystallized ginger, to decorate

Cook's Tip These nutritious, energy-giving squares are a really good choice for packed lunches, as they don't break up too easily.

1 Preheat the oven to 325°F. Grease and line a 7 x 11-inch cake pan.

2 Sift together the flour, baking soda and ground ginger, then stir in the oats. Melt the sugar, margarine and syrup in a saucepan over low heat, then stir into the flour mixture. Beat in the egg and mashed bananas.

3 Spoon into the prepared pan and bake for about 1 hour, until firm to the touch. Allow to cool in the pan, then turn out and cut into squares.

4 Sift the confectioners' sugar into a bowl and stir in just enough water to make a smooth, runny icing. Drizzle the icing over each square and top with a piece of crystallized ginger.

Gingerbread Squares

The flavor of these squares will improve if they are stored in an airtight container for several days before serving.

Makes 16–20

INGREDIENTS

1¼ cups milk
¾ cup light corn syrup
¾ cup molasses
½ cup butter or margarine, chopped
⅓ cup dark brown sugar
4 cups all-purpose flour
½ teaspoon baking soda
1¼ teaspoons ground ginger
4 cups rolled oats
1 egg, beaten
confectioners' sugar for dusting

1 Preheat the oven to 350°F. Grease and line the base of a 8-inch square cake pan. Gently heat together the milk, syrup, molasses, butter or margarine and sugar, stirring until smooth; do not boil.

2 Stir together the flour, baking soda, ginger and oats. Make a well in the center, pour in the egg, then slowly pour in the warmed mixture, stirring to make a smooth batter.

3 Pour the batter into the pan and bake for about 45 minutes, until firm to the touch. Cool slightly in the pan, then cool completely on a wire rack. Cut into squares and dust with confectioners' sugar.

Chocolate Pecan Squares

Makes 16

❧

INGREDIENTS

2 eggs
2 teaspoons vanilla extract
pinch of salt
1¹/₂ cups pecans, coarsely chopped
¹/₂ cup all-purpose flour
4 tablespoons sugar
¹/₂ cup molasses
3 ounces semisweet chocolate,
finely chopped
3 tablespoons butter
16 pecan halves for decorating

❧

1 Preheat the oven to 325°F. Line the bottom and sides of an 8-inch square baking pan with waxed paper and grease lightly.

2 Beat together the eggs, vanilla extract and salt. In another bowl, mix together the pecans and flour. Set both bowls aside.

3 In a saucepan, bring the sugar and molasses to a boil.

4 Remove from the heat and stir in the chocolate and butter and blend thoroughly with a wooden spoon.

5 Mix in the beaten eggs, then fold in the pecan mixture. Pour the batter into the prepared pan and bake for about 35 minutes, until set.

6 Cool in the pan for 10 minutes before unmolding. Cut into 2 inches squares and press pecan halves into the tops while warm. Cool completely on a wire rack.

Raisin Brownies

Makes 16

❧

INGREDIENTS

¹/₂ cup butter or margarine,
chopped
¹/₂ cup cocoa powder
2 eggs
1 cup sugar
1 teaspoon vanilla extract
¹/₃ cup all-purpose flour
³/₄ cup walnuts, chopped
¹/₂ cup raisins

❧

1 Preheat the oven to 350°F. Line an 8-inch square baking pan with waxed paper and grease the paper.

2 Melt the butter or margarine in a small saucepan over low heat. Remove from the heat and stir in the cocoa powder.

3 With an electric mixer, beat together the eggs, sugar, and vanilla extract until light. Add the cocoa mixture and stir to blend.

4 Sift the flour over the cocoa mixture and gently fold in. Add the walnuts and raisins and scrape the batter into the prepared pan. Bake for 30 minutes. Do not overbake.

5 Leave in the pan to cool before cutting into 2-inch squares and removing. The brownies should be soft and moist. Dust with confectioners' sugar before serving.

Chocolate Butterscotch Bars

Makes 24

❦

INGREDIENTS

2 cups all-purpose flour
$^1/_2$ teaspoon baking powder
$^1/_2$ cup unsalted butter, chopped
$^1/_3$ cup light brown sugar
5 ounces semisweet chocolate,
    melted
2 tablespoons ground almonds
For the topping
$^3/_4$ cup unsalted butter
$^1/_2$ cup granulated sugar
2 tablespoons light corn syrup
$^3/_4$ cup condensed milk
1$^1/_4$ cups whole toasted hazelnuts
8 ounces semisweet chocolate,
    chopped

❦

1 Preheat the oven to 325°F. Grease a shallow 12 x 8-inch cake pan. Sift the flour and baking powder into a large bowl. Rub in the butter, then stir in the sugar. Work in the melted chocolate and ground almonds.

2 Press the mixture into the prepared cake pan, prick the surface with a fork and bake for 25–30 minutes, until firm. Allow to cool.

3 To make the topping, mix the butter, sugar, light corn syrup and condensed milk in a saucepan. Heat gently until the butter and sugar have melted. Simmer, stirring occasionally, until golden, then stir in the hazelnuts.

4 Pour over the cooked base and spread out evenly. Allow to set.

5 Melt the chocolate in a bowl over a saucepan of hot water. Spread over the butterscotch layer; allow to set before cutting into bars.

Sour Cream Streusel Bars

A deliciously different tea-time treat.

Makes 12–14

꧂

INGREDIENTS

¹/₂ cup butter
²/₃ cup granulated sugar
3 eggs, at room temperature
1¹/₂ cups all-purpose flour
1 teaspoon baking soda
1 teaspoon baking powder
1 cup sour cream
For the topping
1 firmly packed cup dark brown sugar
2 teaspoons ground cinnamon
1 cup walnuts, finely chopped
4 tablespoons butter, chopped

꧂

1 Preheat the oven to 350°F. Line the bottom of a 9-inch square cake pan with waxed paper and grease the paper.

2 To make the topping, place the brown sugar, cinnamon and walnuts in a bowl. Mix with your fingertips, then add the butter and continue working until the mixture resembles coarse crumbs.

3 Cream the butter with an electric mixer until soft. Add the sugar and continue beating until the mixture is light and fluffy.

4 Add the eggs, one at a time, beating well after each addition.

5 In another bowl, sift the flour, baking soda and baking powder together three times.

6 Fold the dry ingredients into the butter mixture in three batches, alternating with the sour cream. Fold until blended after each addition.

7 Pour half of the batter into the prepared pan and sprinkle over half of the topping.

8 Pour the remaining batter on top and sprinkle over the remaining topping.

9 Bake for 60–70 minutes, until browned. Allow to stand for 5 minutes, then unmold and transfer to a wire rack to cool.

White Chocolate Macadamia Slices

Keep these treats for someone special who will really appreciate

their superb rich flavor and crunchy texture.

Makes 16

❧

INGREDIENTS

1¼ cups macadamia nuts,
blanched almonds or hazelnuts
14 ounces white chocolate,
chopped
⅓ cup dried apricots
⅓ cup unsalted butter
1 teaspoon vanilla extract
3 eggs
scant 1 cup firmly packed light
brown sugar
1 cup self-rising flour

❧

1 Preheat the oven to 375°F. Lightly grease two 8-inch cake pans and line the bottom of each with waxed paper or baking parchment.

2 Coarsely chop the nuts and half the white chocolate, making sure that the pieces are more or less the same size, then cut up the apricots to similar-size pieces.

3 In the top of a double boiler or in a heatproof bowl over a saucepan of hot water, melt the remaining white chocolate over gentle heat with the butter, stirring occasionally until smooth. Remove the bowl from the heat.

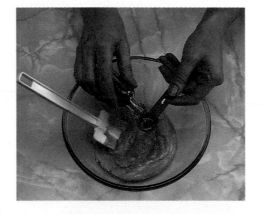

4 Stir in the vanilla extract. Beat the eggs and sugar in a mixing bowl until thick and pale, then beat in the melted chocolate mixture.

5 Sift the flour over the mixture and fold it in evenly. Stir in the nuts, white chocolate and apricots.

6 Spoon the mixture into the prepared pans, smooth the top level and bake for 30–35 minutes.

Cook's Tip It is easier to cut these bars after they have cooled. Use a serrated knife.

Toffee Bars

Makes 32

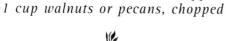

INGREDIENTS

*2 cups firmly packed light
brown sugar
2 cups butter or margarine
2 egg yolks
1½ teaspoons vanilla extract
4 cups all-purpose or
whole wheat flour
pinch of salt
8 ounces milk chocolate, chopped
1 cup walnuts or pecans, chopped*

1 Preheat the oven to 350°F. Grease a 13 x 9 x 2-inch cake pan. Beat together the sugar and butter or margarine until light and fluffy. Beat in the egg yolks and vanilla extract. Stir in the flour and salt.

2 Spread the dough in the prepared cake pan. Bake for 25–30 minutes, until lightly browned. The texture will be soft.

3 Remove from the oven and immediately place the chocolate pieces on the hot cookie base. Let it stand until the chocolate softens, then spread it evenly with a spatula. Sprinkle with the nuts. While still warm, cut into about 2 x 1½-inch bars.

Variation Use chopped pecan nuts instead of walnuts if you prefer, or try a mixture of both.

e Walnut Bars

1 Preheat the oven to 350°F. Grease the sides and bottom of an 8-inch square cake pan.

2 Grind the walnuts with a few tablespoons of the sugar in a food processor, blender or nut grinder.

3 In a bowl, combine the ground walnuts, the remaining sugar, and the flour. Rub in the butter until the mixture resembles coarse crumbs. Alternatively, put all the ingredients in a food processor and process until the mixture resembles coarse crumbs.

4 Pat the walnut mixture into the bottom of the prepared pan in an even layer. Bake for 25 minutes.

5 Meanwhile, to make the topping, melt the butter with the water in a small saucepan over low heat. Beat in the cocoa and sugar.

6 Remove the pan from the heat, stir in the vanilla extract and salt and allow to cool for 5 minutes.

7 Beat in the eggs until blended. Pour the topping evenly over the crust when it is cooked.

8 Return to the oven and bake for about 20 minutes, until set. Place the pan on a wire rack to cool. Cut into 2½ x 1-inch bars and dust with confectioners' sugar. Store in the refrigerator.

Apricot and Almond Fingers

These apricot and almond fingers will stay moist for several days.

Makes 18

INGREDIENTS

2 cups self-rising flour
²/₃ cup firmly packed light brown sugar
¹/₃ cup semolina
1 cup dried apricots, chopped
2 eggs
2 tablespoons malt extract
2 tablespoons honey
4 tablespoons skim milk
4 tablespoons sunflower oil
few drops of almond extract
2 tablespoons slivered almonds

1 Preheat the oven to 325°F. Lightly grease and line an 11 x 7-inch shallow cake pan. Sift the flour into a bowl and add the brown sugar, semolina, dried apricots and eggs. Add the malt extract, honey, milk, sunflower oil and almond extract. Mix well until smooth.

2 Turn the mixture into the prepared cake pan, spread to the edges and sprinkle with the slivered almonds.

3 Bake for 30–35 minutes, until the center of the cake springs back when lightly pressed. Transfer to a wire rack to cool. Remove the paper, place the cake on a board and cut it into 18 slices with a sharp knife.

Apricot Bars

Makes 12

❧

INGREDIENTS

$^1/_2$ cup firmly packed light brown
sugar
$^3/_4$ cup all-purpose flour
$^1/_3$ cup cold unsalted butter,
chopped
For the topping
1 cup dried apricots
1 cup water
grated rind of 1 lemon
$^1/_3$ cup granulated sugar
2 teaspoons cornstarch
$^1/_2$ cup walnuts, chopped

❧

1 Preheat the oven to 350°F. Grease
a 8-inch square cake pan.

2 In a bowl, combine the brown
sugar and flour. Rub in the butter
until the mixture resembles crumbs.

3 Press into the prepared cake pan.
Bake for 15 minutes. Remove
from the oven but leave the oven on.

4 To make the topping, combine the
apricots and water in a saucepan
and simmer for about 10 minutes,
until soft. Strain the liquid and
reserve. Chop the apricots.

5 Return the apricots to the
saucepan and add the lemon rind,
granulated sugar, cornstarch, and
4 tablespoons of the soaking liquid.
Cook for 1 minute.

6 Cool slightly before spreading the
topping over the base. Sprinkle
over the walnuts and continue baking
for 20 minutes more. Allow to cool in
the pan before cutting into bars.

Blueberry Streusel Slices

Makes 30

❧

INGREDIENTS

8 ounces pie-crust pastry
¹/₂ cup all-purpose flour
¹/₄ teaspoon baking powder
3 tablespoons butter or margarine
2 tablespoons fresh white bread crumbs
¹/₃ cup light brown sugar
pinch of salt
4 tablespoons slivered or chopped almonds
4 tablespoons blackberry or other berry jam
scant 1 cup blueberries, fresh or frozen

❧

1 Preheat the oven to 350°F. Roll out the pastry on a lightly floured surface to fit a 7 x 11-inch jelly roll pan. Grease the jelly roll pan.

2 Rub together the flour, baking powder, butter or margarine, bread crumbs, sugar and salt until really crumbly, then mix in the almonds.

3 Place the rolled pastry in the prepared pan. Spread the pastry with the jam, sprinkle with the blueberries, then cover evenly with the streusel topping, pressing down lightly. Bake for 30–40 minutes, lowering the temperature after 20 minutes to 325°F.

4 Remove from the oven. Cut into slices while still hot, then transfer to a wire rack to cool.

Sticky Date and Apple Squares

If possible, allow this mixture to mature for 1–2 days before cutting.

Makes 16

❧

INGREDIENTS

¹/₂ cup margarine
4 tablespoons dark brown sugar
4 tablespoons light corn syrup
²/₃ cup chopped dates
1¹/₃ cups rolled oats
1 cup whole wheat self-rising flour
2 eating apples, peeled, cored and grated
1–2 teaspoons lemon juice
16 walnut halves

❧

1 Preheat the oven to 375°F. Line a 7 or 8-inch square or rectangle loose-bottomed cake pan. In a large saucepan, gently heat the margarine, sugar and syrup together until the margarine has melted completely.

2 Add the dates and cook until they have softened. Gradually work in the oats, flour, apples and lemon juice until well mixed.

3 Spoon into the prepared pan and spread out evenly. Top with the walnut halves. Bake for 30 minutes, then reduce the temperature to 325°F and bake for 10–12 minutes more, until firm to the touch and golden.

4 Cut into squares or bars while still warm if you are going to eat them right away, or wrap in foil when nearly cold and keep for 1–2 days before eating.

Spiced Fig Bars

Makes 48

❦

INGREDIENTS

2 cups dried figs
3 eggs
³/₄ cup granulated sugar
³/₄ cup all-purpose flour
1 teaspoon baking powder
¹/₂ teaspoon ground cinnamon
¹/₄ teaspoon ground cloves
¹/₄ teaspoon grated nutmeg
pinch of salt
³/₄ cup walnuts, finely chopped
2 tablespoons brandy or cognac
confectioners' sugar for dusting

❦

1 Preheat the oven to 325°F. Line a 12 x 8 x 1¹/₂-inch cake pan with waxed paper and grease the paper.

2 With a sharp knife, chop the figs coarsely. Set aside.

3 In a bowl, beat the eggs and sugar until well blended. In another bowl, sift together the dry ingredients, then fold into the egg mixture in several batches.

4 Stir the figs, walnuts and brandy or cognac into the bowl until evenly combined.

5 Scrape the mixture into the prepared cake pan and bake for 35–40 minutes, until the top is firm and brown. It should still be soft underneath. Allow to cool in the pan for 5 minutes, then unmold and transfer to a sheet of waxed paper lightly sprinkled with confectioners' sugar. Cut into bars.

Creamy Lemon Bars

A delicious and luxurious treat, ideal for accompanying a cup of coffee.

Makes 36

❦

INGREDIENTS

¹/₂ cup confectioners' sugar
1¹/₂ cups all-purpose flour
pinch of salt
³/₄ cup butter, chopped
For the topping
4 eggs
1¹/₂ cups granulated sugar
grated rind of 1 lemon
¹/₂ cup fresh lemon juice
³/₄ cup whipping cream
confectioners' sugar for dusting

❦

1 Preheat the oven to 325°F. Grease a 13 x 9-inch cake pan. Sift the sugar, flour and salt into a bowl. Rub in the butter until the mixture resembles coarse crumbs.

2 Press the mixture into the bottom of the prepared cake pan. Bake for about 20 minutes, until golden brown.

3 Meanwhile, to make the topping, beat together the eggs and sugar until blended. Add the lemon rind and juice and mix well.

4 Lightly whip the cream and fold into the egg mixture. Pour over the warm crust, return to the oven, and bake for about 40 minutes, until set. Cool completely before cutting into bars. Dust with confectioners' sugar.

Chocolate Raspberry Macaroon Bars

Any seedless preserve, such as strawberry or apricot, can be substituted for raspberry.

Makes 16–18 bars

INGREDIENTS

¹/₂ cup unsalted butter
¹/₂ cup confectioners' sugar
¹/₄ cup cocoa powder
pinch of salt
1 teaspoon almond extract
1¹/₄ cups all-purpose flour
For the topping
scant ¹/₂ cup seedless raspberry preserves
1 tablespoon raspberry-flavored liqueur
1 cup mini chocolate chips
1¹/₂ cups finely ground almonds
4 egg whites
pinch of salt
1 cup granulated sugar
¹/₂ teaspoon almond essence
¹/₂ cup slivered almonds

2 In a medium bowl, with an electric mixer, beat together the butter, sugar, cocoa and salt until well blended. Add in the almond extract and the flour and mix until the mixture forms a crumbly dough.

3 Turn the dough into the prepared pan and pat firmly over the bottom to make an even layer. Prick the dough with a fork.

4 Bake for 20 minutes, until just set. Remove from the oven and increase the temperature to 375°F.

5 To make the topping, combine the raspberry preserves and raspberry-flavored liqueur in a small bowl. Spread the topping evenly over the chocolate crust, then sprinkle evenly with the chocolate chips.

6 In a food processor fitted with a metal blade, process the almonds, egg whites, salt, sugar and almond extract until well blended and foamy. Gently pour over the jam layer, spreading evenly to the edges of the pan. Sprinkle with slivered almonds.

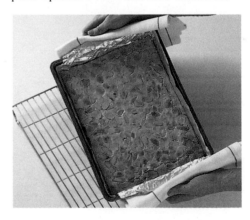

7 Bake for 20–25 minutes more, until the top is golden and puffed. Transfer to a wire rack to cool in the pan for 20 minutes, until firm.

8 Using the edges of the foil, carefully remove the cake from the pan and cool completely. Peel off the foil and, using a sharp knife, cut into bars.

1 Preheat the oven to 325°F. Invert a 9 x 13-inch cake pan. Mold a sheet of foil over the pan and smooth the foil evenly around the corners. Lift off the foil and turn the pan right side up; line with the molded foil. Lightly grease the foil.

Lemon Cheese Bars

Makes 24

❦

INGREDIENTS

1 cup all-purpose flour
¹/₂ cup chopped walnuts
¹/₂ cup light brown sugar
¹/₃ cup unsalted butter
*grated rind and juice of 1 small
lemon*
1 cup full-fat cream cheese
¹/₄ cup granulated sugar
1 tablespoon milk
¹/₂ teaspoon vanilla extract
1 large egg

❦

1 Preheat the oven to 350°F. Grease a 9-inch square cake pan.

2 Beat together the flour, walnuts, brown sugar and butter. Divide the mixture in half. Press one half of the mixture into the prepared cake pan. Bake for 12–15 minutes, until lightly browned. Remove from the oven.

3 Beat together the lemon rind and juice, the cheese and sugar, then beat in the milk, vanilla extract and egg. Spoon over the partly cooked pastry and crumble the remaining mixture evenly over the top. Bake for another 25 minutes, until the top is golden. Transfer to a wire rack to cool, then chill. Cut into bars.

Citrus Spice Bars

Makes 50

❦

INGREDIENTS

*³/₄ cup candied orange peel,
chopped*
¹/₃ cup raisins
5 tablespoons rum
3 tablespoons honey
3 tablespoons molasses
1 egg
1 cup ground almonds
1¹/₂ cups whole wheat flour
¹/₂ teaspoon baking powder
large pinch baking soda
1 teaspoon ground cinnamon
¹/₂ teaspoon ground ginger
*1 cup unblanched almonds,
chopped*
¹/₂ cup sifted confectioners' sugar
about 3 tablespoons orange juice

❦

1 Preheat the oven to 400°F. Lightly grease a 13 x 9-inch cake pan. Place the orange peel, raisins and rum in a bowl, cover and set aside for 1 hour.

2 Pour the honey and molasses into a saucepan and bring to a boil. Set aside to cool, then beat in the egg. Mix together the ground almonds, flour, baking powder, baking soda and spices and stir into the mixture. Stir in the chopped almonds and the rum mixture and form into a dough.

3 Press the dough into the prepared cake pan. Bake for about 20 minutes. Transfer to a wire rack to cool. Sift the confectioners' sugar into a bowl and stir in just enough orange juice to make a spreading consistency. Set aside for 1 hour.

4 Spread the icing over the cake. Decorate if you wish and cut into generous bars.

Chocolate and Coconut Slices

Very simple to make, these slices are deliciously moist and sweet.

Makes 24

❦

INGREDIENTS

*¹/₂ cup butter or margarine,
chopped
6 ounces graham crackers,
crushed
4 tablespoons sugar
pinch of salt
1 cup dried coconut
1¹/₂ cups semisweet chocolate
chips
1 cup sweetened condensed milk
1 cup chopped walnuts*

❦

1 Preheat the oven to 350°F. Melt the butter or margarine in a small saucepan over low heat.

2 In a bowl, combine the crushed graham crackers, sugar, salt and melted butter or margarine. Press the mixture evenly over the bottom of an ungreased 13 x 9-inch baking dish.

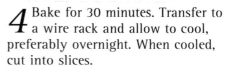

4 Bake for 30 minutes. Transfer to a wire rack and allow to cool, preferably overnight. When cooled, cut into slices.

3 Sprinkle the coconut over the cookie base, then sprinkle over the chocolate chips. Pour the condensed milk evenly over the chocolate. Sprinkle the walnuts on top.

181

Hermits

Makes 30

❧

INGREDIENTS

¾ cup all-purpose flour
1½ teaspoons baking powder
1 teaspoon ground cinnamon
½ teaspoon grated nutmeg
¼ teaspoon ground cloves
¼ teaspoon ground allspice
1½ cups raisins
½ cup butter or margarine
½ cup sugar
2 eggs
½ cup molasses
½ cup walnuts, chopped

❧

1 Preheat the oven to 350°F. Line the bottom and sides of a 13 x 9-inch pan with waxed paper and grease.

2 Sift together the flour, baking powder and spices into a bowl.

3 Place the raisins in another bowl and toss with a few tablespoons of the flour mixture.

4 With an electric mixer, cream together the butter or margarine and sugar, until light and fluffy. Beat in the eggs, one at a time, then the molasses. Stir in the flour mixture, raisins and walnuts.

5 Spread evenly in the prepared cake pan. Bake for 15–18 minutes, until just set. Leave to cool in the pan before cutting into squares or fingers.

Butterscotch Meringue Bars

Makes 12

❧

INGREDIENTS

4 tablespoons butter
1 cup firmly packed dark
brown sugar
1 egg
½ teaspoon vanilla extract
½ cup all-purpose flour
pinch of salt
¼ teaspoon grated nutmeg
For the topping
1 egg white
pinch of salt
1 tablespoon light corn syrup
½ cup granulated sugar
½ cup walnuts, finely chopped

❧

1 Combine the butter and brown sugar in a saucepan and cook until bubbling. Set aside to cool.

2 Preheat the oven to 350°F. Line an 8-inch square cake pan with waxed paper and grease the paper.

3 Beat the egg and vanilla extract into the cooled sugar mixture. Sift over the flour, salt and nutmeg and fold in. Spread over the bottom of the prepared cake pan.

4 To make the topping, beat the egg white with the salt until it holds soft peaks. Beat in the light corn syrup, then the granulated sugar, and continue beating until the mixture holds stiff peaks.

5 Fold in the nuts and spread on top of the mixture in the pan. Bake for 30 minutes. Cut into bars when cool.

Muffins and Scones

Muffins are very easy to make and delicious to eat: to mix the batter, simply use a few swift strokes to stir the liquid ingredients, taking no more than 10–20 seconds. This will leave some lumps. Ignore them. If the batter is mixed for too long, the dough will be tough and the muffins will be coarse-textured and full of tunnels. Rather than being mixed to a smooth pouring consistency, the mixture should come off the spoon in coarse dollops.

Muffins are best eaten when freshly made and still warm, certainly on the day of baking. To re-warm muffins, wrap them loosely in foil and heat for approximately 5 minutes in an oven preheated to 450°F.

The distinction between our biscuits and British scones is very slight, although our bakeries, supermarkets and coffee bars do now offer scones as a breakfast biscuit or muffin, to be split and toasted. In Britain, however, they are an essential part of an afternoon tea, eaten while warm, split, spread with butter and served with cream (preferably clotted) and jam.

Whatever the name, the secrets of their perfect, light, tender scones are not making the dough too wet, handling it quickly and very lightly, and rolling it out with even pressure to the correct thickness – at least ¾ inch, and lastly, preheating the oven to a high temperature, usually about 425°F.

Oatmeal Buttermilk Muffins

Makes 12

INGREDIENTS

1 cup rolled oats
1 cup buttermilk
½ cup butter
½ cup dark brown sugar
1 egg
1 cup all-purpose flour
1 teaspoon baking powder
½ teaspoon baking soda
pinch of salt
¼ cup raisins

Cook's Tip If buttermilk is not available, add 1 teaspoon lemon juice or vinegar to 1 cup of milk. Let the mixture stand a few minutes to curdle before adding it to the oats.

1 In a bowl, combine the oats and buttermilk and allow to soak for 1 hour.

2 Grease 12 muffin pans, or use paper liners. Preheat the oven to 400°F.

3 With an electric mixer, cream the butter and sugar until light and fluffy. Beat in the egg.

4 Sift together the flour, baking powder, baking soda and salt. Stir into the butter mixture, alternating with the oat mixture. Fold in the raisins.

5 Fill the muffin pans two-thirds full. Bake for 20–25 minutes. Transfer to a wire rack to cool.

Pumpkin Muffins

Makes 14

INGREDIENTS

½ cup butter or margarine
¾ cup firmly packed brown sugar
⅓ cup molasses
1 egg, beaten
1 cup cooked or canned pumpkin
1¾ cups all-purpose flour
pinch of salt
1 teaspoon baking soda
1½ teaspoons ground cinnamon
1 teaspoon grated nutmeg
¼ cup currants or raisins

2 With an electric mixer, cream the butter or margarine until soft. Add the sugar and molasses and beat until light and fluffy.

3 Add the egg and pumpkin and stir until well blended.

4 Sift over the flour, salt, baking soda, cinnamon and nutmeg. Fold in until just blended; do not overmix.

5 Fold the currants or raisins into the pumpkin mixture until just evenly combined.

6 Spoon the batter into the prepared muffin pans, filling them two-thirds full.

7 Bake for 12–15 minutes, until the tops spring back when touched lightly. Serve warm or cold.

1 Preheat the oven to 400°F. Grease 14 muffin pans, or use paper liners.

Banana Muffins

Makes 12

INGREDIENTS

*2 cups all-purpose flour
1 teaspoon baking powder
1 teaspoon baking soda
pinch of salt
¹/₂ teaspoon ground cinnamon
¹/₄ teaspoon grated nutmeg
3 large ripe bananas
1 egg
¹/₃ cup dark brown sugar
¹/₄ cup vegetable oil
¹/₄ cup raisins*

1 Preheat the oven to 375°F.

2 Grease 12 muffin pans, or use paper liners.

3 Sift together the flour, baking powder, baking soda, salt, cinnamon and nutmeg. Set aside.

4 With an electric mixer, mash the peeled bananas at moderate speed.

5 Beat the egg, sugar and oil into the mashed bananas.

6 Add the dry ingredients and beat in gradually, on low speed. Mix until just blended. With a wooden spoon, stir in the raisins. Fill the muffin pans two-thirds full.

7 Bake for 20–25 minutes, until the tops spring back when touched lightly. Transfer to a wire rack to cool.

Maple Pecan Muffins

Makes 20

INGREDIENTS

1¼ cups pecans
2½ cups all-purpose flour
1 teaspoon baking powder
1 teaspoon baking soda
pinch of salt
¼ teaspoon ground cinnamon
½ cup granulated sugar
⅓ cup firmly packed light
brown sugar
3 tablespoons maple syrup
⅔ cup butter
3 eggs
1¼ cups buttermilk
60 pecan halves to decorate

Variation For Pecan Spice Muffins, substitute an equal quantity of molasses for the maple syrup. Increase the cinnamon to ½ teaspoon, and add 1 teaspoon ground ginger and ½ teaspoon grated nutmeg, sifted with the flour and other dry ingredients.

1 Preheat the oven to 350°F. Grease 20 muffin pans, or use paper liners.

2 Spread the pecans on a baking sheet and toast in the oven for 5 minutes. Allow to cool, then chop coarsely and set aside.

3 In a bowl, sift together the flour, baking powder, baking soda, salt and cinnamon. Set aside.

4 In a large mixing bowl, combine the granulated sugar, light brown sugar, maple syrup and butter. Beat with an electric mixer until light and fluffy.

5 Add the eggs, one at a time, beating to incorporate thoroughly after each addition.

6 Pour half of the buttermilk and half of the dry ingredients into the butter mixture, then stir until blended. Repeat with the remaining buttermilk and dry ingredients.

7 Fold the chopped pecans into the batter. Fill the muffin pans two-thirds full. Top with the pecan halves.

8 Bake for 20–25 minutes, until puffed up and golden. Allow to stand for 5 minutes before transferring to a wire rack to cool.

Raspberry Muffins

Low-fat buttermilk gives these muffins a light and spongy texture.

They are delicious to eat at any time of day.

Makes 10–12

INGREDIENTS

2¹⁄₂ cups all-purpose flour
1 tablespoon baking powder
¹⁄₂ cup sugar
1 egg
1 cup buttermilk
4 tablespoons sunflower oil
1 cup raspberries

Variation Cranberry Muffins: a breakfast treat that is not too sweet.

3 cups all-purpose flour
1 teaspoon baking powder
pinch of salt
¹⁄₂ cup sugar
2 eggs
²⁄₃ cup milk
4 tablespoons corn oil
finely grated rind of 1 orange
1 cup cranberries

1 Preheat the oven to 375°F. Line 12 deep muffin pans with paper liners. Mix the flour, baking powder, salt and caster sugar together. Lightly beat the eggs with the milk and oil.

2 Add the liquids to the dry ingredients and blend to make a smooth batter. Divide the mixture between the muffin pans and bake for 25 minutes, until risen and golden. Allow to cool in the pans for a few minutes, and serve warm or cold.

1 Preheat the oven to 400°F. Arrange 12 paper liners in deep muffin pans. Sift the flour and baking powder into a mixing bowl, stir in the sugar, then make a well in the center.

2 Mix the egg, buttermilk and sunflower oil together in a bowl, pour into the flour mixture and mix quickly until just combined.

3 Add the raspberries and lightly fold in with a metal spoon. Spoon the mixture into the paper liners.

4 Bake for 20–25 minutes, until golden brown and firm in the center. Transfer to a wire rack and serve warm or cold.

Double Chocolate Chip Muffins

These marvelous muffins are packed with chunky semisweet and white

chocolate chips.

Makes 16

INGREDIENTS

3¹⁄₂ cups all-purpose flour
1 tablespoon baking powder
2 tablespoons cocoa powder
¹⁄₂ cup firmly packed dark
brown sugar
2 eggs
²⁄₃ cup sour cream
²⁄₃ cup milk
4 tablespoons sunflower oil
6 ounces white chocolate
6 ounces semisweet chocolate
cocoa powder for dusting

Cook's Tip If sour cream is not available, sour ²⁄₃ cup light cream by stirring in 1 teaspoon lemon juice and letting the mixture stand until thickened.

1 Preheat the oven to 375°F. Place 16 paper muffin liners in muffin pans or popover pans. Sift the flour, baking powder and cocoa into a bowl and stir in the sugar. Make a well in the center.

2 In a separate bowl, beat the eggs with the sour cream, milk and oil, then stir into the well in the dry ingredients. Beat well, gradually incorporating the flour mixture to make a thick and creamy batter.

Variation Make sure you use good quality chocolate with a high cocoa content. Vary the proportions of semisweet and white chocolate, or add in milk chocolate if you prefer.

3 Finely chop the chocolate and stir into the batter mixture.

4 Spoon the mixture into the muffin liners, filling them almost to the top. Bake for 25–30 minutes, until well risen and firm to the touch. Transfer to a wire rack to cool, then dust with cocoa powder.

Chocolate Walnut Muffins

Walnuts and chocolate are a delicious combination.

Makes 12

INGREDIENTS

³/₄ *cup unsalted butter, chopped*
5 ounces semisweet chocolate,
chopped
1 cup granulated sugar
¹/₄ *cup firmly packed dark*
brown sugar
4 eggs
1 teaspoon vanilla extract
¹/₄ *teaspoon almond extract*
³/₄ *cup all-purpose flour*
1 cup walnuts, chopped

1 Preheat the oven to 350°F. Grease muffin pans, or use paper liners.

2 Melt the butter with the chocolate in the top of a double boiler or a heatproof bowl over a saucepan of hot water. Transfer to a large mixing bowl.

3 Stir both the sugars into the chocolate mixture. Mix in the eggs, one at a time, then add the vanilla and almond extract.

4 Sift over the flour and fold in until evenly combined.

5 Stir the walnuts evenly into the chocolate mixture.

6 Fill the muffin pans almost to the top and bake for 30–35 minutes. Allow to stand for 5 minutes before transferring to a wire rack.

Chocolate Chip Muffins

Use the best quality chocolate chips you can find.

Makes 10

INGREDIENTS

¹/₂ *cup butter or margarine*
¹/₃ *cup granulated sugar*
2 tablespoons dark brown sugar
2 eggs
1¹/₂ cups all-purpose flour
1 teaspoon baking powder
¹/₂ *cup milk*
1 cup semisweet chocolate chips

1 Preheat the oven to 375°F. Grease 10 muffin pans, or use paper liners.

2 With an electric mixer, cream the butter or margarine until soft. Add both sugars and beat until light and fluffy. Beat in the eggs, one at a time.

3 Sift the flour and baking powder, twice. Fold into the butter mixture, alternating with the milk.

4 Divide half of the mixture between the muffin pans. Sprinkle several chocolate chips on top, then cover with a spoonful of batter.

5 Bake for about 25 minutes, until lightly colored. Allow to stand for 5 minutes before transferring to a wire rack to cool.

Banana and Nut Buns

Use walnut pieces instead of pecans if you prefer.

Makes 8

INGREDIENTS

1¼ cups all-purpose flour
1½ teaspoons baking powder
¼ cup butter or margarine
¾ cup sugar
1 egg
1 teaspoon vanilla extract
3 medium bananas, mashed
½ cup chopped pecans
⅓ cup milk

1 Preheat the oven to 375°F. Grease eight muffin pans.

2 Sift the flour and baking powder into a small bowl. Set aside.

3 With an electric mixer, cream together the butter or margarine and the sugar. Add the egg and vanilla extract and beat until fluffy. Mix in the bananas.

4 Add the pecans. With the mixer on low speed, beat in the flour mixture alternately with the milk. Spoon the mixture into the prepared pans. Bake for 20–25 minutes, until a skewer or cake tester inserted in the center of a bun comes out clean.

5 Allow to cool in the muffin pans for 10 minutes. Unmold onto the wire rack. Cool for 10 minutes longer before serving.

Fruit and Cinnamon Buns

Makes 8

INGREDIENTS

1 cup all-purpose flour
1 tablespoon baking powder
pinch of salt
scant ½ cup light brown sugar
1 egg
¾ cup milk
3 tablespoons vegetable oil
2 teaspoons ground cinnamon
1 cup fresh or thawed frozen
blueberries, or black currants

1 Preheat the oven to 375°F. Grease eight muffin pans.

2 With an electric mixer, beat together the first eight ingredients until smooth.

3 Fold the blueberries or black currants into the other ingredients until just evenly combined.

4 Spoon the mixture into the muffin pans, filling them two-thirds full. Bake for about 25 minutes, until a skewer or cake tester inserted in the center of a bun comes out clean.

5 Allow to cool in the muffin pans, on a wire rack, for 10 minutes, then transfer the buns to the wire rack and allow to cool completely.

Carrot Muffins

Makes 12

INGREDIENTS

¾ cup margarine
½ cup dark brown sugar
1 egg
1 tablespoon water
2 cups grated carrots
1¼ cups all-purpose flour
1 teaspoon baking powder
½ teaspoon baking soda
1 teaspoon ground cinnamon
¼ teaspoon grated nutmeg
pinch of salt

1 Preheat the oven to 350°F. Grease 12 muffin pans, or use paper liners.

2 With an electric mixer, cream the margarine and sugar until light and fluffy. Beat in the egg and water.

3 Stir the grated carrots into the creamed mixture until evenly combined. Sift over the flour, baking powder, baking soda, cinnamon, nutmeg and salt. Stir to blend evenly.

4 Spoon the batter into the prepared muffin pans, filling them almost to the top.

5 Bake for about 35 minutes, until the tops spring back when touched lightly. Allow to stand for 10 minutes before transferring to a wire rack to cool.

Dried Cherry Muffins

If you can't find dried cherries, use the same amount of dried cranberries.

Makes 16

INGREDIENTS

1 cup plain yogurt
1 cup dried cherries
½ cup butter
¾ cup sugar
2 eggs
1 teaspoon vanilla extract
1¾ cups all-purpose flour
2 teaspoons baking powder
1 teaspoon baking soda
pinch of salt

1 In a mixing bowl, combine the yogurt and cherries. Cover and let stand for 30 minutes.

2 Preheat the oven to 350°F. Grease 16 muffin pans, or use paper liners.

3 With an electric mixer, cream together the butter and sugar until light and fluffy.

4 Add the eggs, one at a time, beating well after each addition. Add the vanilla extract and the cherry mixture and stir to blend. Set aside.

5 In another bowl, sift together the flour, baking powder, baking soda and salt. Fold into the cherry mixture in three batches; do not overmix.

6 Fill the prepared muffin pans two-thirds full. Bake for about 20 minutes, until the tops spring back when touched lightly. Transfer to a wire rack to cool.

Prune Muffins

Muffins with prunes are moist, delicious breakfast treats.

Makes 12

INGREDIENTS

1 egg
1 cup milk
¼ cup vegetable oil
¼ cup granulated sugar
2 tablespoons dark brown sugar
2 cups all-purpose flour
2 teaspoons baking powder
pinch of salt
¼ teaspoon grated nutmeg
¾ cup cooked pitted prunes, chopped

1 Preheat the oven to 400°F. Grease 12 muffin pans or use paper liners.

2 Break the egg into a mixing bowl and beat with a fork. Beat in the milk and oil.

3 Stir the sugars into the egg mixture. Set aside. Sift the flour, baking powder, salt and nutmeg into a mixing bowl. Make a well in the center, pour in the egg mixture and stir. The batter should be slightly lumpy.

4 Gently fold the prunes into the batter until just evenly distributed. Fill the prepared muffin pans two-thirds full.

5 Bake for about 20 minutes, until golden brown. Allow to stand for 10 minutes before transferring to a wire rack. Serve warm or at room temperature.

Yogurt Honey Muffins

Makes 12

INGREDIENTS

4 tablespoons butter
5 tablespoons honey
1 cup plain yogurt
1 egg
grated rind of 1 lemon
¼ cup lemon juice
1 cup all-purpose flour
1 cup whole wheat flour
1½ teaspoons baking soda
pinch of grated nutmeg

Variation For Walnut Yogurt Honey Muffins, add ½ cup chopped walnuts, folded in with the flour. This makes a more substantial muffin.

1 Preheat the oven to 375°F. Grease 12 muffin pans, or use paper liners.

2 In a saucepan, melt the butter and honey. Remove from the heat and set aside to cool slightly.

3 In a bowl, beat together the yogurt, egg, lemon rind and juice. Add the butter and honey mixture. Set aside.

4 In another bowl, sift together the dry ingredients. Fold the dry ingredients into the yogurt mixture just to blend.

5 Fill the prepared muffin pans two-thirds full. Bake for 20–25 minutes, until the tops spring back when touched lightly. Allow to cool in the pan for 5 minutes before transferring to a wire rack. Serve warm or at room temperature.

Raisin Bran Muffins

Makes 15

❦

INGREDIENTS

4 tablespoons butter or margarine
²/₃ cup all-purpose flour
¹/₂ cup whole wheat flour
1¹/₂ teaspoons baking soda
pinch of salt
1 teaspoon ground cinnamon
¹/₂ cup bran
¹/₂ cup raisins
¹/₃ cup dark brown sugar
¹/₄ cup granulated sugar
1 egg
1 cup buttermilk
juice of ¹/₂ lemon

❦

1 Preheat the oven to 400°F. Grease 15 muffin pans, or use paper liners.

2 Place the butter or margarine in a saucepan and melt over low heat. Set aside. In a mixing bowl, sift together the all-purpose flour, whole wheat flour, baking soda, salt and cinnamon.

3 Add the bran, raisins and sugars and stir until blended. In another bowl, mix together the egg, buttermilk, lemon juice and melted butter or margarine.

4 Add the buttermilk mixture to the dry ingredients and stir lightly and quickly until just moistened; do not mix until smooth.

5 Spoon the batter into the prepared muffin pans, filling them almost to the top. Bake for 15–20 minutes, until golden. Serve warm or at room temperature.

Raspberry Crumble Muffins

Makes 12

INGREDIENTS

1½ cups all-purpose flour
2 teaspoons baking powder
pinch of salt
1 teaspoon ground cinnamon
¼ cup granulated sugar
¼ cup firmly packed light
brown sugar
½ cup butter, melted
1 egg
½ cup milk
1¼ cups fresh raspberries
grated rind of 1 lemon
For the crumble topping
¼ cup pecans, finely chopped
¼ cup firmly packed
dark brown sugar
3 tablespoons all-purpose flour
1 teaspoon ground cinnamon
3 tablespoons butter, melted

1 Preheat the oven to 350°F. Grease 12 muffin pans, or use paper liners. Sift the flour, baking powder, salt and cinnamon into a bowl. Add the sugars, and stir to blend.

2 Make a well in the center of the mixture. Place the butter, egg and milk in the well and mix until just combined. Stir in the raspberries and lemon rind. Spoon the batter into the prepared muffin pans, filling them almost to the top.

3 To make the crumble topping, mix the pecans, dark brown sugar, flour and cinnamon in a bowl. Stir in the melted butter.

4 Spoon some of the crumble over each muffin. Bake for about 25 minutes. Transfer to a wire rack to cool slightly. Serve warm.

Nutty Muffins with Walnut Liqueur

Walnut liqueur gives a lift to these big crunchy muffins.

Makes 12–14

INGREDIENTS

2 cups all-purpose flour
4 teaspoons baking powder
1/2 teaspoon apple pie spice
pinch of salt
2/3 cup firmly packed light
brown sugar
3/4 cup chopped walnuts
4 tablespoons butter, melted
2 eggs
3/4 cup milk
2 tablespoons walnut liqueur
For the topping
2 tablespoons dark brown sugar
1/4 cup chopped walnuts

1 Preheat the oven to 400°F. Grease 12–14 muffin pans or deep bun pans, or use paper muffin liners supported in muffin pans. Sift the flour, baking powder, apple pie spice and salt into a mixing bowl, then stir in the sugar and chopped walnuts.

2 In a cup, combine the melted butter, eggs, milk and liqueur.

3 Pour the butter mixture into the dry mixture and stir for just long enough to combine the ingredients. The batter should be lumpy.

4 Fill the muffin or bun pans two-thirds full, then top with a sprinkling of dark brown sugar and walnuts. Bake for 15 minutes, until the muffins are golden brown. Leave in the pans for a few minutes, then transfer to a wire rack to cool.

Apple and Cinnamon Muffins

These spicy muffins are quick and easy to make and are perfect for serving for a special breakfast.

Makes 6

INGREDIENTS

1 egg, beaten
3 tablespoons granulated sugar
¹/₂ cup milk
¹/₄ cup butter, melted
1¹/₄ cups all-purpose flour
1¹/₂ teaspoons baking powder
pinch of salt
¹/₂ teaspoon ground cinnamon
2 small eating apples, peeled, cored and finely chopped
For the topping
3 tablespoons raw sugar
1 teaspoon ground cinnamon

Cook's Tip Do not overmix the muffin mixture – it should be lumpy.

3 Bake for 30–35 minutes, until well risen and golden. Transfer to a wire rack to cool.

1 Preheat the oven to 400°F. Line six large muffin pans with paper liners. Mix the egg, sugar, milk and melted butter in a large bowl. Sift in the flour, baking powder, salt and cinnamon. Add the chopped apple and mix coarsely.

2 Spoon the mixture into the prepared muffin pans. To make the topping, mix the raw sugar with the cinnamon. Sprinkle over the uncooked muffins. Bake for 30–35 minutes, until well risen and golden. Transfer to a wire rack to cool.

Pineapple and Cinnamon Pancakes

Making the batter with pineapple juice instead of milk cuts down on fat and adds to the taste.

Makes 24

INGREDIENTS

1 cup self-rising whole wheat flour
1 cup self-rising white flour
1 teaspoon ground cinnamon
1 tablespoon sugar
1 egg
1¼ cups pineapple juice
½ cup dried pineapple, chopped

Cook's Tip Eat these right away with applesauce for a healthy treat.

1 Preheat a griddle, heavy-bottomed frying pan or an electric frying pan. Put the whole wheat flour in a mixing bowl. Sift in the white flour, add the cinnamon and sugar and make a well in the center. Add the egg with half of the pineapple juice.

2 Gradually incorporate the flour to make a smooth batter. Beat in the remaining juice with the chopped pineapple.

3 Grease the griddle or pan. Drop tablespoons of the batter onto the surface, leaving them until they bubble and the bubbles begin to burst.

4 Turn the drop pancakes with a metal spatula and cook until the underside is golden brown. Continue to cook in successive batches.

Chocolate Chip Banana Pancakes

These delicious moist pancakes are topped with cream and toasted almonds.

Makes 16

INGREDIENTS

2 ripe bananas
⅞ cup milk
2 eggs
1¼ cups self-rising flour
¼ cup ground almonds
1 tablespoon granulated sugar
pinch of salt
1½ tablespoons semisweet
chocolate chips
butter for frying
For the topping
⅔ cup whipping cream
1 tablespoon confectioners' sugar
½ cup toasted slivered almonds,
to decorate

Cook's Tip For banana and blueberry pancakes, replace the chocolate with 1 cup fresh blueberries. These pancakes are also delicious when accompanied by ice cream.

1 In a bowl, mash the bananas with a fork, combine with half of the milk and beat in the eggs. Sift in the flour, ground almonds, sugar and salt. Make a well in the center and pour in the remaining milk. Add the chocolate chips and stir to produce a thick batter.

2 Heat one pat of butter in a non-stick frying pan. Spoon the pancake mixture into heaps, allowing room for them to spread. When the mixture starts to bubble, turn the pancakes over and cook briefly on the other side.

3 Lightly whip the cream with the confectioners' sugar to sweeten it. Spoon the cream onto the pancakes and decorate with slivered almonds.

Teatime Scones

Makes 16

❧

INGREDIENTS

2 cups all-purpose flour
pinch of salt
¹/₂ teaspoon baking soda
1 teaspoon cream of tartar
2 tablespoons butter
about ²/₃ cup milk or buttermilk

❧

Variation These traditional favorites can be varied by adding:
1–2 tablespoons of chocolate chips or 1–2 teaspoons ground cinnamon.

1 Preheat the oven to 425°F. Flour a baking sheet. Sift the flour, salt, baking soda and cream of tartar into a bowl.

2 Rub in the fat until the mixture resembles fine bread crumbs. Gradually stir in just enough milk to make a light, spongy dough.

3 Turn the dough onto a lightly floured surface and knead until smooth. Roll to 1 inch thick. Cut into rounds with a floured 2-inch cutter (or a 1¹/₂-inch cutter for cocktail savories).

4 Place the scones on the prepared baking sheet and brush the tops with milk. Bake for 7–10 minutes, until the scones are well risen and golden brown.

Lavender Scones

Serve these scented scones warm, with plum jam and whipped cream.

Makes 12

❧

INGREDIENTS

2 cups all-purpose flour
1 tablespoon baking powder
4 tablespoons butter
¹/₄ cup sugar
2 teaspoons fresh lavender florets or 1 teaspoon dried culinary lavender, roughly chopped
about ³/₄ cup milk

❧

1 Preheat the oven to 425°F. Grease a baking sheet. Sift together the flour and baking powder. Rub the butter into the dry ingredients until the mixture resembles bread crumbs.

2 Stir in the sugar and lavender florets, reserving a pinch of lavender to sprinkle on the top of the scones before baking them.

3 Add enough milk to make a soft, sticky dough. Pull the mixture together and then turn the dough onto a well-floured work surface.

4 Shape the dough into a circle, and roll out to a 1 inch depth. Using a floured cutter, stamp out 12 scones.

5 Place on the prepared baking sheet. Brush the tops with a little milk and sprinkle with the reserved lavender.

6 Bake for 10–12 minutes, until golden.

Sunflower Golden Raisin Biscuits

Makes 10–12

❧

INGREDIENTS

2 cups self-rising flour
1 teaspoon baking powder
2 tablespoons margarine
2 tablespoons raw sugar
¹/₃ cup golden raisins
2 tablespoons sunflower seeds
²/₃ cup plain yogurt
about 2–3 tablespoons milk

❧

1 Preheat the oven to 450°F. Lightly oil a baking sheet. Sift the flour and baking powder into a bowl and rub in the margarine. Stir in the sugar, golden raisins and half of the sunflower seeds, then mix in the plain yogurt.

2 Add just enough milk to the mixture to make a soft dough.

3 Roll out on a lightly floured surface to about ³/₄ inch thick. Cut into 2¹/₂-inch rounds with a floured cutter and lift onto the baking sheet.

4 Brush the biscuits with milk and sprinkle them with the reserved sunflower seeds.

5 Bake for 10–12 minutes, until well risen and golden brown. Transfer to a cooling rack. Serve while still warm, with jam, butter or low-fat spread.

Whole Wheat Scones

Whole wheat scones are both delicious and healthy.

Makes 16

〰

INGREDIENTS

¼ *cup cold butter*
2 *cups whole wheat flour*
1 *cup all-purpose flour*
2 *tablespoons sugar*
pinch of salt
2½ *teaspoons baking soda*
2 *eggs*
¾ *cup buttermilk*
¼ *cup raisins*

〰

1 Preheat the oven to 400°F. Grease and flour a large baking sheet.

2 Cut the butter into small pieces. Combine the dry ingredients in a bowl. Add the butter and rub in until the mixture resembles coarse crumbs. Set aside.

3 In another bowl, beat together the eggs and buttermilk. Set aside 2 tablespoons for glazing.

4 Stir the remaining egg mixture into the dry ingredients until it just holds together. Stir in the raisins.

5 Roll out the dough about ¾ inch thick. Stamp out circles with a floured cookie cutter. Place on the prepared baking sheet and brush with the glaze.

6 Bake for 12–15 minutes, until golden. Allow to cool slightly before serving. Split in half with a fork while still warm and spread with butter and jam, if wished.

Orange Raisin Scones

Makes 16

〰

INGREDIENTS

2 *cups all-purpose flour*
1½ *tablespoons baking powder*
⅓ *cup sugar*
pinch of salt
5 *tablespoons butter, chopped*
grated rind of 1 large orange
⅓ *cup raisins*
½ *cup buttermilk*
milk for glazing

〰

1 Preheat the oven to 425°F. Grease and flour a large baking sheet.

2 Combine the dry ingredients in a large bowl. Add the butter and rub in until the mixture resembles coarse crumbs.

3 Add the orange rind and raisins. Gradually stir in the buttermilk to form a soft dough.

4 Roll out the dough on a floured surface to about ¾ inch thick. Stamp out circles with a floured cookie cutter.

5 Place on the prepared baking sheet and brush the tops with milk. Bake for 12–15 minutes, until golden. Serve hot or warm, with butter or whipped cream, and jam.

Cook's Tip For light, delicate scones, handle the dough as little as possible. If you wish, split the scones when cool and toast them. Butter them while they are still hot.

Cookies
for Kids

This chapter includes recipes that are suitable for children to eat, like Gingerbread Teddy Bears, and recipes that children can make themselves. Quite a number of these recipes do not even need to be baked, such as Date Crunch, Fruit and Nut Clusters and Marshmallow Krispie Cakes.

Kids – before you embark on a cookie-making session, there are a few guidelines that will help you towards ending up with a batch to be proud of. Start by washing and drying your hands. If your hair is long, tie it back. Wear an apron both to protect your clothes from the food and to protect the food from your clothes. Make sure the kitchen surfaces are clean and tidy before you begin.

Next, read through the recipe from start to finish very carefully so you can make sure you have all the ingredients and equipment you will need, and so you have a clear idea of what you are going to be doing and in what order. Now you can get out all the equipment you'll need and assemble and carefully measure all the ingredients.

Follow the recipe exactly and take your time. Avoid any distractions or interruptions, such as friends or brothers or sisters coming in, or the radio playing, in case you make a mistake or forget where you are in the recipe. If you are in any doubt about anything at all, at any time, or feel you need a hand, don't hesitate to ask a grown-up.

Chewy Fruit Muesli Slice

An easy recipe that needs just measuring, mixing and baking.

Makes 8

INGREDIENTS

¹/₂ cup dried apricots, chopped
1 eating apple, cored and grated
1¹/₄ cups Swiss-style muesli
²/₃ cup apple juice
1 tablespoon soft margarine

1 Preheat the oven to 375°F. Place all the ingredients in a large bowl and mix well.

2 Press the mixture into an 8-inch nonstick cake pan and bake for 35–40 minutes, until lightly browned and firm.

3 Mark the muesli slice into eight wedges and allow to cool in the pan.

Oat and Apricot Clusters

Here is a variation on an old favorite that children can easily make themselves,
so have plenty of the dried fruits and nuts ready for them to add.

Makes 12

❧

INGREDIENTS

4 tablespoons butter or margarine
3 tablespoons honey
$\frac{1}{2}$ cup rolled oats
$\frac{1}{3}$ cup chopped dried apricots
1 tablespoon dried banana chips
1 tablespoon dried
shredded coconut
2–3 cups cornflakes or Rice
Krispies

❧

1 Place the butter or margarine and honey in a small saucepan and warm over low heat, stirring.

2 Add the oats, apricots, banana chips, coconut and cornflakes or Rice Krispies and mix well.

3 Spoon the mixture into 12 paper baking liners, piling it up roughly. Transfer to a baking sheet, or a tray, and chill until set and firm.

Cook's Tip The ingredients can be changed according to what's in your pantry – try peanuts, pecans, raisins or dates.

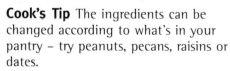

219

Fruit and Nut Clusters

This is a fun, no-cook recipe that children will like to make and eat.

Makes 24

🌿

INGREDIENTS

8 ounces white chocolate
¹/₃ cup sunflower seeds
¹/₂ cup slivered almonds
¹/₃ cup sesame seeds
¹/₃ cup raisins
1 teaspoon ground cinnamon

🌿

1 Break the white chocolate into small pieces. Put the chocolate into a heatproof bowl over a saucepan of hot water on low heat. Do not allow the water to touch the base of the bowl, or the chocolate may become too hot.

2 Alternatively, put the chocolate in a microwave-proof container and heat it on Medium for 3 minutes. Stir the melted chocolate until it is smooth and glossy.

3 Mix the remaining ingredients together, pour in the chocolate and stir well.

4 Using a teaspoon, spoon the mixture into paper baking liners and allow to set.

Marshmallow Krispie Cakes

Makes 45

❦

INGREDIENTS

9 ounce bag of toffees
4 tablespoons butter
3 tablespoons milk
1 cup marshmallows
6 cups Rice Krispies

❦

1 Lightly brush an 8 x 13-inch roasting pan with a little oil. Put the toffees, butter and milk in a saucepan and heat gently, stirring until the toffees have melted.

2 Add the marshmallows and cereal, and stir until well mixed and the marshmallows have melted.

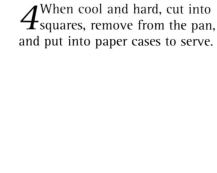

4 When cool and hard, cut into squares, remove from the pan, and put into paper cases to serve.

3 Spoon into the prepared roasting pan, level the surface and allow to set. Cut into squares, put into paper baking liners and serve.

Date Crunch

Makes 24

INGREDIENTS

8-ounce package graham crackers
¹/₃ cup butter
2 tablespoons light corn syrup
¹/₂ cup pitted dates, finely chopped
3 ounces golden raisins
5 ounces milk or semisweet
chocolate, chopped

Cook's Tip For an alternative topping, drizzle 3 ounces melted white and 3 ounces melted dark chocolate over.

1 Line a 7-inch square shallow cake pan with foil. Put the crackers in a plastic bag and crush coarsely with a rolling pin.

2 Gently heat the butter and syrup in a small saucepan until the butter has melted.

3 Stir in the crushed crackers, the dates and golden raisins and mix well. Spoon into the prepared pan, press flat with the back of a spoon and chill for 1 hour.

4 Melt the chocolate in a heatproof bowl, over a saucepan of hot water, stirring until smooth. Spoon over the cookie mixture, spreading evenly with a spatula. Chill until set. Lift the foil out of the cake pan and peel away. Cut the crunch into 24 pieces and arrange on a plate.

Peanut Cookies

Packing up a picnic? Got a birthday party coming up?

Make sure some of these nutty cookies are on the menu.

Makes 25

INGREDIENTS

1 cup butter
2 tablespoons smooth peanut butter
1 cup confectioners' sugar
½ cup cornstarch
2 cups all-purpose flour
1 cup unsalted peanuts

1 Put the butter and peanut butter in a bowl and beat together. Add the confectioners' sugar, cornstarch and all-purpose flour and mix together to make a soft dough.

2 Preheat the oven to 350°F. Lightly oil two baking sheets. Roll the mixture into 25 small balls, using your hands, and place on the baking sheets. Leave plenty of room for the cookies to spread.

3 Press the tops of the balls of dough flat, using either the back of a fork or your fingertips.

4 Press a few of the peanuts into each of the cookies. Bake for 15–20 minutes, until lightly browned. Allow to cool for a few minutes before lifting them carefully onto a wire rack with a metal spatula.

Cook's Tip Make monster cookies by rolling bigger balls of dough. Remember to leave plenty of room on the baking sheets for them to spread, though.

Chocolate Crackle-Tops

Older children will enjoy making these distinctive cookies.

Makes 38

❦

INGREDIENTS

*7 ounces semisweet chocolate,
chopped
scant 1/2 cup unsalted butter
1/2 cup granulated sugar
3 eggs
1 teaspoon vanilla extract
scant 2 cups all-purpose flour
1/4 cup unsweetened cocoa
1/2 teaspoon baking powder
pinch of salt
1 1/2 cups confectioners' sugar for
coating*

❦

1 In a medium saucepan over low heat, melt the chocolate and butter together until smooth, stirring frequently.

2 Remove from the heat. Stir in the sugar, and continue stirring for 2–3 minutes, until the sugar dissolves. Add the eggs one at a time, beating well after each addition; stir in the vanilla.

3 Into a bowl, sift together the flour, cocoa, baking powder and salt. Gradually stir into the chocolate mixture in batches, until just blended.

4 Cover the dough and refrigerate for at least 1 hour, until the dough is cold and holds its shape.

5 Preheat the oven to 325°F. Grease two or more large baking sheets. Place the confectioners' sugar in a small, deep bowl. Using a small ice-cream scoop or round teaspoon, scoop cold dough into small balls and, between the palms of your hands, roll into 1 1/2 inch balls.

6 Drop each ball into the confectioners' sugar and roll until heavily coated. Remove with a slotted spoon and tap against the side of the bowl to remove excess sugar. Place on the prepared baking sheets 1 1/2 inches apart.

7 Bake the cookies for 10–15 minutes, until the tops feel slightly firm when touched. Remove the baking sheet to a wire rack for 2–3 minutes. With a metal spatula, remove the cookies to a wire rack to cool completely.

Chocolate Dominoes

A recipe for children to eat rather than make. Ideal for birthday parties.

Makes 16

❧

INGREDIENTS

¾ cup soft margarine
¾ cup granulated sugar
1¼ cups self-rising flour
¼ cup cocoa powder, sifted
3 eggs
For the topping
¾ cup butter
¼ cup cocoa powder
2½ cups confectioners' sugar
a few licorice strips and 4-ounce
package M & M's, for decoration

❧

Variation To make Traffic Light Cakes, omit the cocoa and add an extra 3 tablespoons all-purpose flour. Omit cocoa from the icing and add an extra 4 tablespoons confectioners' sugar and ½ teaspoon vanilla extract. Spread over the cakes and decorate with red, yellow and green candied cherries to look like traffic lights.

1 Preheat the oven to 350°F. Lightly brush a 7 x 11-inch baking pan with a little oil and line the base of the pan with waxed paper.

2 Put all the cake ingredients in a bowl and beat until smooth.

3 Spoon into the prepared cake pan and level the surface with a spatula.

4 Bake for 30 minutes, until the cake springs back when pressed with the fingertips.

5 Cool in the pan for 5 minutes, then loosen the edges with a knife and transfer to a wire rack. Peel off the paper and allow the cake to cool. Turn the cake onto a chopping board and cut into 16 bars.

6 To make the topping, place the butter in a bowl, sift in the cocoa and confectioners' sugar and beat until smooth. Spread the topping evenly over the cakes with a spatula.

7 Add a strip of licorice to each cake, decorate with M & M's for domino dots and arrange the cakes on a serving plate.

Lemony Peanut Pairs

For those who don't like peanut butter, use buttercream or chocolate-and-nut spread instead.

Makes 8–10

INGREDIENTS

¹/₄ *cup light brown sugar*
¹/₄ *cup soft margarine*
1 teaspoon grated lemon rind
³/₄ *cup whole wheat flour*
¹/₄ *cup chopped crystallized
pineapple*
*2 tablespoons smooth peanut
butter*
*sifted confectioners' sugar for
dusting*

1 Preheat the oven to 375°F.
Grease a baking sheet. Cream the
sugar, margarine and lemon rind
together. Work in the flour and knead
until smooth.

2 Roll out thinly and cut into
rounds, then place on the baking
sheet. Press on pieces of pineapple
and bake for 15–20 minutes. Cool.
Sandwich together with peanut
butter, dust with confectioners' sugar.

Ginger Cookies

If your children enjoy cooking with you, mixing and rolling the dough, or cutting out

different shapes, this is the ideal recipe to let them practice on.

Makes 16

INGREDIENTS

²/₃ *cup brown sugar*
¹/₂ *cup soft margarine*
pinch of salt
few drops of vanilla extract
1¹/₄ cups whole wheat flour
1 tablespoon cocoa, sifted
2 teaspoons ground ginger
a little milk
*icing glaze and candied cherries,
to decorate*

1 Preheat the oven to 375°F. Grease
a baking sheet. Cream together
the sugar, margarine, salt and vanilla
extract until very soft and light.

2 Work in the flour, cocoa and
ginger, adding a little milk, if
necessary, to bind the mixture.
Knead lightly on a floured surface
until smooth.

3 Roll out the dough to about
¹/₄ inch thick. Stamp out shapes
using floured cookie cutters and place
on the prepared baking sheet.

4 Bake the cookies for 10–15
minutes. Allow to cool on the
baking sheets until firm, then transfer
to a wire rack to cool completely.
Decorate with glaze icing and
candied cherries.

Gingerbread Jungle

Snappy cookies in animal shapes, which can be decorated in your own style.

Makes 14

🌿

INGREDIENTS

1¹/₂ cups self-rising flour
¹/₂ teaspoon baking soda
¹/₂ teaspoon ground cinnamon
2 teaspoons granulated sugar
¹/₄ cup butter
3 tablespoons light corn syrup
¹/₂ cup confectioners' sugar
1–2 teaspoons water

🌿

Cook's Tip Any cutters can be used with the same mixture. Obviously, the smaller the cutters, the more cookies you will make.

1 Preheat the oven to 375°F. Lightly oil two baking sheets.

2 Put the flour, baking soda, cinnamon and granulated sugar in a bowl and mix together. Melt the butter and syrup in a saucepan. Pour over the dry ingredients.

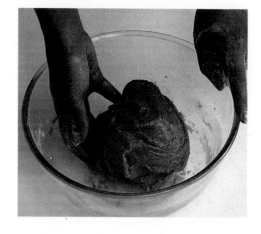

3 Mix together well and then use your hands to pull the mixture together to make a dough.

4 Turn onto a lightly floured surface and roll out to about ¹/₄ inch thick.

5 Use floured animal cutters to cut shapes from the dough and arrange on the prepared baking sheets, leaving enough room between them to rise.

6 Press the trimmings back into a ball, roll it out and cut more shapes. Continue until all the dough is used. Bake for 8–12 minutes, until lightly browned.

7 Allow to cool slightly, before transferring to a wire rack with a metal spatula. Sift the confectioners' sugar into a small bowl and add enough water to make a fairly soft icing.

8 Spoon the icing into a pastry bag fitted with a small, plain nozzle and pipe decorations on the cookies.

Sweet Necklaces

These are too complicated for young children to make but are ideal as novelty Christmas

presents. Arrange in a pretty, tissue-lined box or tin for presentation.

Makes 12

☙

INGREDIENTS

1 quantity Lebkuchen mixture
1 quantity icing glaze
pink food coloring
selection of small candies
6 yards fine pink, blue or white
ribbon

☙

1 Preheat the oven to 350°F. Grease two large baking sheets. Roll out slightly more than half of the Lebkuchen mixture on a lightly floured surface to a thickness of ¼ inch.

3 Gather the trimmings together with the remaining dough. Roll the dough under the palms of your hands, to make a thick sausage about 1 inch in diameter. Cut in ½-inch slices. Using the skewer, make a hole in the center of each. Put on the second baking sheet.

4 Bake for about 8 minutes, until slightly risen and just beginning to color. Remove from the oven and, while still warm, re-make the skewer holes because the gingerbread will have spread slightly during baking. Allow to cool on a wire rack.

5 Put half the icing glaze in a paper icing bag and snip off a tip. Use to pipe outlines around the stars. Color the remaining icing with the pink coloring. Spoon into a paper icing bag fitted with a star nozzle.

6 Cut the candies into smaller pieces and use to decorate the cookies. Set aside to harden.

2 Cut out stars using a floured 1-inch star cutter. Transfer to a baking sheet, spacing them evenly. Taking care not to distort the shape of the stars, make a large hole in the center of each, using a metal or wooden skewer.

7 Cut the ribbon into 20-inch lengths. Thread a selection of the cookies onto each ribbon.

Chocolate-Tipped Cookies

Get those cold hands wrapped around a steaming hot drink,

and tuck into chocolate-tipped cookies.

Makes 22

❦

INGREDIENTS

¹⁄₂ cup margarine
3 tablespoons confectioners'
sugar, sifted
1¹⁄₄ cups all-purpose flour
few drops vanilla extract
3 ounces semisweet chocolate,
chopped

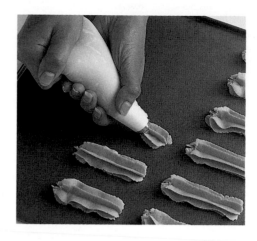

1 Preheat the oven to 350°F. Lightly grease two baking sheets. Put the margarine and confectioners' sugar in a bowl and cream them together until very soft. Mix in the flour and vanilla extract.

2 Spoon the mixture into a large pastry bag fitted with a large star nozzle and pipe 4–5 inch lines on the prepared baking sheets. Cook for 15–20 minutes, until pale golden brown. Allow to cool slightly before lifting onto a wire rack. Let the cookies cool completely.

3 Put the chocolate in a small heatproof bowl. Stand in a saucepan of hot, but not boiling, water until it melts. Dip both ends of each cookie into the chocolate, put back on the rack and allow to set. Serve with hot chocolate topped with whipped cream.

Cook's Tip Make round cookies if you prefer, and dip half of each cookie in the melted chocolate.

Five-Spice Fingers

Light, crumbly cookies with an unusual Chinese five-spice flavoring.

Makes 28

❧

INGREDIENTS

½ cup margarine
½ cup confectioners' sugar
1 cup all-purpose flour
2 teaspoons Chinese five-spice
powder
grated rind and juice of ½ orange

❧

1 Preheat the oven to 350°F. Lightly grease two baking sheets. Put the margarine and half the confectioners' sugar in a bowl and beat with a wooden spoon, until the mixture is smooth and creamy.

2 Add the flour and five-spice powder and beat again. Spoon the mixture into a large pastry bag fitted with a large star nozzle.

3 Pipe short lines of mixture, about 3 inches long, on the prepared baking sheets. Leave enough room for them to spread.

4 Bake for 15 minutes, until lightly brown. Allow to cool slightly, before transferring to a wire rack with a metal spatula.

5 Sift the remaining confectioners' sugar into a small bowl and stir in the orange rind. Add enough juice to make a thin icing. Brush over the cookies while they are still warm.

Cook's Tip These cookies are delicious served with ice cream or creamy desserts.

Gingerbread Teddy Bears

These endearing teddy bears, dressed in striped pajamas, would make a perfect gift for friends of any age. If you can't get a large cutter, make smaller bears or use a traditional gingerbread-man cutter. You might need some help from an adult with the decorating.

Makes 6

❧

INGREDIENTS

3 ounces white chocolate, chopped
6 ounces ready-to-roll white sugar paste
blue food coloring
1 ounce semisweet or milk chocolate
For the gingerbread
1½ cups all-purpose flour
¼ teaspoon baking soda
pinch of salt
1 teaspoon ground ginger
1 teaspoon ground cinnamon
⅓ cup unsalted butter, chopped
⅓ cup sugar
2 tablespoons maple or corn syrup
1 egg yolk, beaten

❧

1 To make the gingerbread, sift together the flour, baking soda, salt and spices into a large bowl. Rub the butter into the flour until the mixture resembles fine bread crumbs.

2 Stir in the sugar, syrup and egg yolk and mix to a firm dough. Knead lightly. Wrap and chill for 30 minutes.

3 Preheat the oven to 350°F. Grease two large baking sheets. Roll out the gingerbread dough on a floured surface and cut out teddy bears, using a floured 5-inch cookie cutter.

4 Transfer to the prepared baking sheets and bake for 10–15 minutes, until just beginning to color around the edges. Leave on the baking sheets for 3 minutes and then transfer to a wire rack.

5 Melt half of the white chocolate. Put in a paper icing bag and snip off the tip. Make a neat template for the bears' clothes: draw an outline of the cutter onto paper, finishing at the neck, halfway down the arms and around the legs.

6 Thinly roll the sugar paste on a surface dusted with confectioners' sugar. Use the template to cut out the clothes, and secure them to the bears with the melted chocolate.

7 Use the sugar paste trimmings to add ears, eyes and snouts. Dilute the blue coloring with a little water and use it to paint the striped pajamas.

8 Melt the remaining white chocolate and the plain or milk chocolate in separate bowls over saucepans of hot water. Put in separate paper piping bags and snip off the tips. Use the white chocolate to pipe a decorative outline around the pajamas and use the semisweet or milk chocolate to pipe the faces.

Cookie
Treats
and Gifts

Everyone has times when they feel the need to indulge themselves. If your fancy is for something rich and sweet, or if you want to give someone a treat, delve into the next few pages and you will find just the ticket.

A delicious gift that is homemade is always received with delight, and cookies, because they have a special place in nearly everyone's heart, are doubly acceptable, even if they are simple. Of course, if the cookies require a little extra skill, such as Honey and Nut Clusters, they will be

received with even more pleasure. With homemade cookies, it is so easy to hit upon an ideal gift every time, whether it is just a small token or something very special.

The slightly more complicated cookies are also particularly therapeutic to make and provide a rewarding job for a quiet morning or afternoon, or a rainy day when you want to bring a little sunshine into your life. However, none of the recipes in this chapter are beyond the bounds of a reasonably competent home cook.

Chocolate Nut Clusters

These are an ideal way to end a dinner party, or to give as a gift for a special friend.

Makes 30

❧

INGREDIENTS

*2¼ cups heavy cream
2 tablespoons unsalted butter,
chopped
1½ cups light corn syrup
scant 1 cup granulated sugar
½ cup firmly packed light
brown sugar
pinch of salt
1 tablespoon vanilla extract
3¾ cups hazelnuts, pecans,
walnuts, brazil nuts or unsalted
peanuts, or a combination
14 ounces semisweet chocolate,
chopped
2 tablespoons vegetable shortening*

❧

1 Lightly oil two baking sheets. In a heavy-bottomed saucepan over medium heat, cook the first six ingredients until the sugars dissolve and the butter melts. Bring to a boil and cook, stirring frequently, for about 1 hour, until the caramel reaches 238°F (soft ball stage) on a sugar thermometer.

2 Place the bottom of the saucepan in a pan of cold water to stop cooking, or transfer the caramel to a smaller saucepan. Cool slightly, then stir in the vanilla extract.

3 Stir the nuts into the caramel until well-coated. Using an oiled tablespoon, drop spoonfuls of the nut mixture onto the prepared sheets, about 1 inch apart. If the mixture hardens, return to the heat to soften.

4 Refrigerate the clusters for 30 minutes, until firm and cold, or leave in a cool place until hardened.

Cook's Tip If you do not have a sugar thermometer, you can test cooked sugar for "soft ball stage" by spooning a small amount into a bowl of cold water: when taken out it should form a soft ball when rolled between finger and thumb.

5 Using a metal palette knife, transfer the clusters to a wire rack placed over a baking sheet to catch drips.

6 In a medium saucepan, over a low heat, melt the chocolate and vegetable shortening, stirring until smooth. Cool slightly.

7 Spoon chocolate over each cluster, being sure to cover completely. Alternatively, using a fork, dip each cluster into chocolate and lift out, tapping on the edge of the saucepan to shake off excess.

8 Place on the wire rack over the baking sheet. Allow to set for 2 hours, until hardened.

Striped Cookies

These biscuits may be made in different flavors and colors and look wonderful tied in bundles or packed into boxes. Eat them with ice cream or light desserts.

Makes 25

❧

INGREDIENTS

*1 ounce white chocolate, melted
red and green food coloring
2 egg whites
¹/₃ cup sugar
¹/₂ cup all-purpose flour
4 tablespoons unsalted butter, melted*

❧

1 Preheat the oven to 375°F. Line two baking sheets with baking parchment. Divide the melted chocolate in half and add a little food coloring to each half to color the chocolate red and green. Using two waxed paper icing bags, fill with each color chocolate and fold down the tops. Snip off the points.

2 Place the egg whites in a bowl and beat until stiff. Add the sugar gradually, beating well after each addition, to make a thick meringue. Add the flour and melted butter and beat until smooth.

3 Drop four **separate** teaspoonfuls of the **mixture** onto the prepared baking sheets **and** spread into thin rounds. Pipe **lines** or zigzags of green and red **chocolate** over each round.

4 Bake one **sheet** at a time for 3–4 minutes, until pale golden in color. Loosen **the** rounds with a metal spatula and **return** to the oven for a few seconds to soften. Have two or three lightly **oiled** wooden spoon handles at **hand**.

5 Taking **one** round cookie out of the oven **at** a time, roll it around a spoon **handle** and leave for a few seconds to **set**. Repeat to shape the remaining cookies. Put the second sheet of cook**ies** in to bake.

6 When the cookies are set, slip them off the spoon handles onto a wire rack. Repeat with the remaining mixture and the red and green chocolate until all the mixture has been used, baking only one sheet of cookies at a time. If the cookies are too hard to shape, simply return them to the oven for a few seconds to soften.

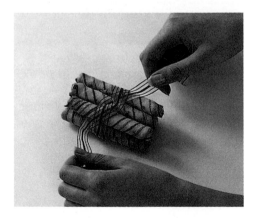

7 When the cookies are cold, tie them together with colored ribbon and pack into boxes, tins or glass jars.

Almond Fingers

A very simple Middle Eastern sweet that is especially popular in Arab countries.

Makes 40–50

❦

INGREDIENTS

1¾ *cups ground almonds*
½ *cup ground pistachios*
¼ *cup granulated sugar*
1 *tablespoon rose water*
½ *teaspoon ground cinnamon*
12 *sheets of filo pastry, defrosted*
½ *cup butter, melted*
confectioners' sugar for dusting

❦

1 Preheat the oven to 325°F. Butter a baking sheet. Mix together the almonds, pistachios, sugar, rose water and cinnamon.

2 Cut each sheet of filo pastry into four rectangles. Work with one at a time, and cover the remaining rectangles with a damp dish towel.

3 Brush one rectangle with melted butter, and place a teaspoon of the nut filling in the center.

4 Fold the sides and roll into a finger shape. Continue until all the filling has been used.

5 Place the "fingers" on the baking sheet and bake for 30 minutes. Transfer to a wire rack to cool, then dust with confectioners' sugar.

Basbousa

These delicious Middle Eastern coconut sweets can be served

either hot as a dessert or cold with tea.

Makes 12

❦

INGREDIENTS

½ *cup unsalted butter*
¾ *cup sugar*
½ *cup all-purpose flour*
1¼ *cups semolina*
1½ *cups grated coconut*
¾ *cup milk*
1 *teaspoon baking powder*
1 *teaspoon vanilla extract*
almonds, to decorate
For the syrup
½ *cup sugar*
⅔ *cup water*
1 *tablespoon lemon juice*

❦

1 To make the syrup, place sugar, water and lemon juice in a saucepan, bring to a boil, simmer for 6–8 minutes. Allow to cool, then chill.

2 Preheat the oven to 350°F. Melt the butter in a saucepan. Add the remaining ingredients and mix thoroughly.

3 Pour the cake mixture into a shallow baking pan, flatten the top and bake for 30–35 minutes.

4 Remove the Basbousa from the oven and cut into diamond-shaped pieces. Pour the cold syrup evenly over the top and decorate with an almond placed in each center.

Semolina and Nut Halva

Semolina is a popular ingredient in many desserts and pastries in the Eastern Mediterranean. Here it provides a sponge cake for soaking up a deliciously fragrant spicy syrup.

Makes 20–24

❦

INGREDIENTS

¹⁄₂ cup unsalted butter
¹⁄₂ cup sugar
finely grated rind of 1 orange
2 tablespoons orange juice
3 eggs
1 cup semolina
2 teaspoons baking powder
1 cup ground hazelnuts
¹⁄₂ cup unblanched hazelnuts, toasted and chopped
¹⁄₂ cup blanched almonds, toasted and chopped
shredded rind of 1 orange
For the syrup
1¹⁄₂ cups sugar
2¹⁄₄ cups water
2 cinnamon sticks, halved
juice of 1 lemon
4 tablespoons orange flower water

❦

1 Preheat the oven to 425°F. Grease and line the bottom of a deep 9-inch square heavy-based cake pan.

2 Lightly cream the butter in a bowl. Add the sugar, orange rind and juice, the eggs, semolina, baking powder and hazelnuts and beat the ingredients together until smooth.

3 Turn into the prepared pan and level the surface. Bake for 20–25 minutes, until just firm and golden. Leave to cool in the pan.

4 To make the syrup, put the sugar in a heavy-bottomed saucepan with the water and cinnamon sticks. Heat until the sugar has dissolved.

5 Bring to a boil and boil hard for 5 minutes. Measure half the syrup in a pitcher and add the lemon juice and orange flower water to it. Pour over the halva. Reserve the remainder of the syrup in the pan.

6 Leave the halva in the pan until the syrup is absorbed, then turn it out onto a plate and cut diagonally into diamond-shaped portions. Sprinkle with the nuts.

7 Boil the remaining syrup until slightly thickened, then pour it over the halva. Sprinkle the shredded orange rind over the cake and serve with lightly whipped cream.

Jeweled Elephants

These stunningly robed elephants make a lovely gift for all ages, or an edible decoration for a special occasion. If you make holes in them before baking, you could use them as original Christmas tree decorations.

Makes 10

INGREDIENTS

1 quantity Lebkuchen mixture
1 quantity Icing Glaze
red food coloring
8 ounces ready-to-roll sugar paste
small candy-covered
chocolates or chews
gold dragees

3 Knead some red food coloring into half of the sugar paste. Roll a little red sugar paste under your fingers into ropes. Secure them around the feet and tips of the trunk, using icing from the bag. Shape more red sugar paste into flat oval shapes, about ¾ inch long, and stick them to the elephants' heads. Shape smaller ovals and secure them at the top of the trunks.

5 Pipe ½-inch tassels around the edges. Pipe dots of white icing at the tops of the trunks, around the necks and at the tops of the tails and also use it to draw small eyes. Halve the small chocolates and press the halves into the sugar paste, above the tassels. Decorate the headdress, candies and white sugar paste with gold dragees, securing them with dots of icing. Set aside for several hours, to harden.

1 Preheat the oven to 350°F. Grease two large baking sheets. Make a paper template for the elephant. Roll out the Lebkuchen mixture. Use the template and a sharp knife to cut out elephant shapes. Space them slightly apart on the baking sheet and bake for 3 minutes and then transfer to a wire rack to cool.

2 Put a little Icing Glaze in a paper icing bag fitted with a fine nozzle. Alternatively, cut off the tip of the bag to make a nozzle.

4 Roll out the white sugar paste. Cut out circles, using a 2½-inch cookie cutter. Secure to the elephants' backs with royal icing so that the edge of the sugar paste is about 1 inch above the top of the legs. Trim off the excess paste around the top of the white sugar paste shapes.

Index

Index